A Practical
Guide to Logical
Data Modeling

Other McGraw-Hill Books of Interest

To order or receive additional information on these or any other McGraw-Hill titles, in the United States please call 1-800-822-8158. In other countries, contact your local McGraw-Hill representative.

MH93

A Practical
Guide to Logical
Data Modeling

George Tillmann

McGraw-Hill, Inc.

New York   San Francisco   Washington, D.C.   Auckland   Bogotá
Caracas   Lisbon   London   Madrid   Mexico City   Milan
Montreal   New Delhi   San Juan   Singapore
Sydney   Tokyo   Toronto

Library of Congress Cataloging-in-Publication Data

Tillmann, George.
  A practical guide to logical data modeling / George Tillmann.
    p.   cm. — (Systems Design and Implementation Series)
  Includes index.
  ISBN 0-07-064615-5
  1. Data base design.   2. Data structures (Computer science)
I. Title.
QA76.9.D26T55   1993
005.74—dc20   93-28715
                                                             CIP

1 2 3 4 5 6 7 8 9 0   DOC/DOC   9 9 8 7 6 5 4 3

ISBN 0-07-064615-5

*The sponsoring editor for this book was Jeanne Glasser, the technical
editor was Fran Reich, the editing supervisor was Ruth W. Mannino,
and the production supervisor was Pamela A. Pelton. It was set in
Century Schoolbook by North Market Street Graphics.*

Printed and bound by R. R. Donnelley & Sons Company.

To Teresa, Carolyn, Ralph, Catherine, and especially Gloria

and in memory of George

Contents

Chapter 1. Modeling: The Keeper of the Vision   5

The current system development landscape is littered with confusing terms and misapplied concepts. This chapter sorts out the issues and describes the role of logical data modeling in the system development life cycle.

Chapter 2. Underlying Principles   21

The fundamental principles that form the basis or justification for the data modeling function are defined and examined.

Chapter 3. Reviewing the Basics   29

Fundamental to any discussion of logical data modeling is a firm understanding of its concepts and conventions. This chapter is useful for the neophyte who needs to learn the basics as well as for the experienced modeler who can use it to spruce up rusty skills and, more importantly, to become familiar with common definitions and terminology. The text also presents the diagramming and conceptual conventions of a number of data modeling tools.

Chapter 4. More about the Entity-Relationship Approach   43

A complement to the previous discussion, this chapter explores more fully what the in-the-field modeler must know about the entity-relationship approach.

Chapter 5. Building the Logical Data Model   63

As a practical guide to gathering the details that are needed to develop the logical data model, this chapter covers the techniques for interviewing users and verifying models as well as common misconceptions about the process and how to avoid costly mistakes.

This chapter introduces a set of guidelines, presented as a number of rules, which are linked to the principles discussed in Chapter 2. The combination of Chapters 2 and 6 is a starter set of rules to follow on a logical data modeling project.

The rules of thumb presented in this chapter are, in effect, best practices. The entries consist of topics that would catch the eye of the experienced modeler and are particularly relevant for modelers who are called upon to review the data model. However, rules of thumb should be viewed with a certain amount of caution. Although they are useful, they are not necessarily applicable in all situations. They are to be read, judged, and applied accordingly.

This chapter outlines what the logical data modeler must do to ensure that the physical database designer has the necessary information to develop efficient and effective database schemas or file layouts.

Object-oriented analysis, design, databases, and programming languages are a recent edition to the war on poor system development productivity. This chapter demonstrates how logical data modeling concepts fit into object-oriented theory and modeling.

Modern methodologies, techniques such as logical data modeling, and tools offer new approaches to system development and maintenance. However, one ingredient is critical to the success of any project, namely, creativity. Although in danger of being lost in a whirl of technology, the need for the creativity of the system analyst/designer has not changed. This chapter examines the problem and gives some thought to the solution.

Appendix A presents a simple system design and illustrates how a number of popular data modeling and Computer Aided Software Engineering (CASE) tools would handle the situation.

Appendix B contains a checklist of principles, guidelines, and rules of thumb.

Appendix C contains a reading list of a number of useful articles and books on the subject. The list is short and practical.

Foreword

Data modeling is one of the most important steps in information system development. The most widely accepted approach to data modeling is the Entity-Relationship (E-R) approach. This book gives a clear, yet thorough treatment of many important data modeling and E-R concepts from a practitioner's point of view.

Although quite a few books have been published on data modeling or the E-R approach, most of them stress the elegance of the theory and the glorified benefits of the data model. There is a need for a practical book with less emphasis on the consistency and completeness of the concepts and greater emphasis on identifying which concepts are useful in practice (not just in theory or on paper). Mr. George Tillmann is one of the best persons to write this kind of book. He has many years of practical data modeling experience at a large international management and technology consulting firm. He is the one down in the "trenches" trying to make data modeling deliver the results/benefits promised by the theoreticians/visionaries in this field. In this book he tells us which concepts will work and which will not.

In addition to synthesizing useful ideas from existing literature, this book also contains some innovative data modeling concepts. For example, the discussion on whether it is possible to have a mandatory recursive relationship (Chapter 4) is very intriguing and, based on my knowledge, has not been published elsewhere. Therefore, this book not only provides you with concepts that really work in practice, but it also gives you some of the author's new ideas and insights.

I hope that you will enjoy reading the book as I did. I sincerely believe and hope that you will benefit from the ideas herein, and wish you great success in your next data modeling project!

Peter Chen
Chen & Associates, Inc.
Baton Rouge, Louisiana

Acknowledgments

Many people have contributed their time and efforts to making this book a reality. Thanks to Vaidyanathan "Chandy" Chandrashekhar, Donna DeMartino, Claus Nehmzow, Arnold Schiemann, Joe Simon, and Mary Jo Ubriaco for their technical help in the sometimes black art of data modeling. Special thanks to Fran Reich for the many hours she spent making the manuscript readable. Her efforts were invaluable. Also many thanks to the partners and staff of Booz•Allen & Hamilton Inc. for their support and encouragement.

Trademarks

ADW and Application Development Workbench are registered trademarks of KnowledgeWare, Inc.

ER-Designer and ER-Modeler are trademarks of Chen & Associates, Inc.

ERwin/ERX is a trademark, and Logic Works is a registered trademark, of Logic Works, Inc.

Excelerator is a registered trademark of INTERSOLV Corporation.

Information Engineering Methodology is a registered trademark of James Martin & Co.

MacFlow is a trademark of Mainstay.

MacFlow Symbol Sampler is a trademark of Synergistic Applications, Inc.

Macintosh is a registered trademark of Apple Computer, Inc.

PROplanner is a trademark of Holland Systems Corporation.

STRADIS is a registered trademark of Structured Solutions, Inc.

System Architect is a trademark of Popkin Software and Systems Inc.

A Practical
Guide to Logical
Data Modeling

Introduction

[Alice came to a fork in the road and saw a
Cheshire cat in a tree.]
'Would you tell me, please, which way I ought
to go from here?'
'That depends a good deal on where you want
to go,' said the Cat.
'I don't know much where,' said Alice.
'Then it doesn't matter which way you go,'
said the Cat."   LEWIS CARROLL

"When you come to a fork in the road, take it."
                                    YOGI BERRA

Logical data modeling involves the analysis and documentation of information that an organization uses in the pursuit of its function. Historically, data modeling was the focus of a select group of individuals whose profession and avocation were the management of data, while processes and algorithms were the domain of the majority of analysts and designers. This division of system development activities between data and process was intentional.

Today, proponents of more recent system development methodologies, such as Information Engineering, and techniques, such as object-oriented analysis and design, criticize this approach. The "separate but equal" view of data and process is giving way to a more integrated "one analyst does all" model. Thus developers, who might have years of process training and experience but almost no data training, are being forced to build both process and data models—an activity for which they are intellectually, and perhaps emotionally, not prepared. Even well-intentioned designers have run into problems building a logical data model.

Although data modeling basics are well established and widely accepted, little has been written about the "how to" of building a model. Traditional texts have provided the theoretical foundations of the various flavors of data modeling; however, they have all but ignored a discussion of the practical difficulties of resolving disagreements, e.g., is an object an entity type or role, or what is the best approach for normalizing the model. In the confusion, the benefits of logical modeling can quickly trickle away.

Purpose

The purpose of this book is to provide both the data modeling neophyte and the seasoned pro with a practical handbook on logical data modeling. In contrast to most data modeling books that are conceptual or academic in nature, this book offers a practical "what do we do now?" set of answers. Its three objectives are to

- Present a tool-independent overview of the basics of logical data modeling.

- Introduce a common set of guidelines or "rules" to follow when data modeling, the adoption of which can go a long way to reducing, if not eliminating, interpretation problems during a project. The rules can be followed as is, or modified to accommodate a given situation or organization. Regardless of the approach, all the rules that will be applied should be established before a project gets under way so that they will be free of context influences.

- Review how some of the popular data modeling and computer-aided software engineering (CASE) tools support logical data modeling concepts and graphics.

Approach

This book takes a "best practices" approach. As applied to this subject, best practices are a set of recommendations that tell developers what actions they should take or avoid to maximize the achievement of their goals. These recommendations are based on years of experience in the field, participation in projects, and observations of the successful actions taken by seasoned professionals.

These advisory statements are not necessarily complete or, arguably, consistent. Clearly, no rule applies to every situation, nor is there only one rule to follow in a given situation. The developer might find that two or more rules apply to a given instance, which could yield different results. Thus, best practices are limited in their ability to guide the professional.

In spite of these difficulties, this portfolio of advice is useful and provides valuable information, though it should neither replace nor diminish the decision process. Developers cannot rely on best practices to make their decisions for them. The responsibility is still theirs. However, the wise developer would consult these rules before charting a course of action.

This portfolio of advice comes in three varieties:

- Principles that form the axioms of the best practices
- Guidelines that should always be followed to remain consistent with the principles
- Rules of thumb, which are consistent with the principles but should be situationally applied

Since the concern of this book is with applied data modeling for the application developer (not theoretical data modeling for the academic), certain decisions were made which, it is hoped, will facilitate the practicing developer's application of data modeling. For example, the book

- Consolidates the ANSI conceptual and external data models into the logical data model.
- Focuses on the entity-relationship approach to data modeling, which is by far the major force in logical data modeling in the United States and in most parts of the world.
- Includes some extended entity–relationship (semantic data modeling) concepts, such as generalization, because of their importance to data modeling, their object-oriented significance, and/or their availability on data modeling and CASE tools.
- Excludes other concepts, such as classification, because they have not yet worked their way into the system development mainstream and/or because they do not provide sufficient value to warrant their inclusion.
- Includes some concepts only implicitly since they are found and explained in other concepts. For example, aggregation is included implicitly in the discussion about entities and attributes. Thus, the explicit treatment of this concept is unnecessary.
- Treats relational theory as a model for a database management system (DBMS) construct and not the more semantic RM/T data model.
- Presents a few new concepts to lessen confusion, such as the replacement of modality for optionality in Chap. 3. Likewise, the concepts of asymmetrical and symmetrical relationships (Chaps. 4 and 7) are

introduced to correct some confusion that recently appeared in some publications.

Some may disagree with this approach, i.e., some may feel the book goes into too much detail for the practicing data modeler, while others may believe the discussion is not rigorous enough. However, since the objective is to bring data modeling out of the realm of the academic and into the arena of the professional system developer, some academic distractions are deliberately omitted, and emphasis is placed on the issues that the practicing developer will face. Hopefully, after all is considered, the average data modeler is better served by this detailed examination of data modeling constructs.

1

Modeling:
The Keeper of the Vision

"It isn't that they can't see the solution.
It is that they can't see the problem."
                        C. K. CHESTERTON

"The problem is not whether machines think
but whether men do."   B. F. SKINNER

Systems have and will continue to become increasingly complex. In the early 1970s, an average application consisted of perhaps 20 to 50 programs and three or four major data files. In the 1990s, even moderately sized applications can involve more than 200 programs, 20 or more record types, and tens or even hundreds of thousands of lines of code.

As could be expected, the role of project managers has also evolved. In the past, one of their responsibilities was to keep the vision of the overall system *in their mind*, thus ensuring that the components of an application remained faithful to the purpose of the system. That is no longer possible given today's large and complex systems. The vision must reside elsewhere. And this new, more complex vision must be partitioned into bite-sized chunks, so that individuals can grasp at least part of the system without destroying its placement in the whole. Out of this complexity was born the concept of modeling.

A common definition of the word model is an abstract representation of a subject that looks and/or behaves like all or part of the original. Although it is not real, the model can be physical, such as a mockup of the space shuttle, a drawing, or blueprint, or it can be conceptual, such as the mathematical formulas used for weather forecasting. Modeling is the process of creating the abstract representation of a subject. A subject is modeled so that it can be studied more cheaply (a scale model of an airplane in a wind tunnel) or at a particular moment in time (weather forecasting), or manipulated, modified, and altered without disrupting the original (economic models).

Applying this definition in today's computer world, the vision of an overall system model is, in actuality, a series of models that represent processes, data, and the movement of information throughout an organization. These models reside on paper as text and diagrams or in machines as codes, and ideally they are understandable by humans and computers alike.

Process Modeling

Since the 1970s, considerable emphasis has been placed on formalizing the construction of models as well as on the analysis and design steps of application development. The most significant results of these efforts are the structured analysis and structured design approaches which help the developer ensure that

- End-user needs are adequately understood and documented.
- Critical issues are surfaced.
- Development staff have relevant input to support the successful completion of the analysis, design, and programming steps.

Using structured analysis, developers build a logical process model, i.e., a logical picture of the organizational processes—the basic objects in the organization and how they interact with each other and with the outside world. Consideration of physical issues, such as hardware and software, are postponed until a later phase. Once the developer understands and documents what the end user wants, attention is then turned to how to deliver the desired system. Using structured design techniques during the physical design process, developers construct a physical process model (see Fig. 1.1). Programmers can then use this model as a guide for coding.

The discipline of structured analysis and design gives the everyday developer access to the experience and wisdom of the expert. Specifically, structured techniques can provide the developer with

- Useful system building advice based on actual experience.
- Discipline (e.g., "Do this before doing that") to ensure that all important steps are completed and in the correct sequence.
- Examples of successful analysis and design deliverables.

Structured analysis and design techniques are excellent if the objectives are to understand the processes of a business and to translate

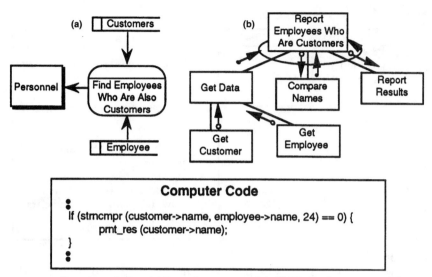

Figure 1.1   Process modeling. (*a*) Logical process model. (*b*) Physical process model.

them into the directions that a programmer needs to write code. But, as good as these techniques are, they are incomplete. What is missing is the equally important emphasis on data.

Data Modeling vs. Process Modeling

Although process modeling does an excellent job of representing business functions, it does not do as well at communicating (and modeling) the data an organization needs and uses—the things that database designers want and need to know. There are four different, though interconnected, reasons for this.

1. *Processes are dynamic by nature, while data is typically static.* When users talk about their workplace, they usually focus on organizational processes. The picture they paint is one of movement and action, e.g., invoices arrive, orders are taken, products are shipped to customers. Process modeling must record these movements, and the processes they describe generally have action-oriented names such as "Validate Customer Credit Status" or "Calculate Balance." By contrast, data is quite static. A customer name does not move or initiate some change or action.

2. *Processes are more volatile than data.* The processes in an organization are more prone to change than data, and they typically change at a much faster rate. The way an organization processed orders last year is not necessarily the way it will process them this year, and no

TABLE 1.1.   Process vs. Data Characteristics

Processes	Data
• Dynamic (involves movement)	• Static
• The definition changes frequently	• The definition rarely changes
• Principal user is the programmer	• Principal user is the database designer
• Best documentation methods show algorithms, movement of data, and flow of control	• Best documentation methods show data definitions and data relationships

one knows how they will be processed next year. However, while the way orders are processed might change every year, the data involved with the orders probably has not (and may not be) changed for many years.

Given this constant evolution of processes, process modeling techniques must be able to accommodate change. However, the data an organization uses, or, more accurately, the definition of the data an organization uses, changes far less frequently. Even when data does change, the change is more likely to affect only a few objects, not masses of objects as often occurs with process changes. By separating the documentation of volatile processes from the more stable data, the changes in one area are prevented from affecting the other.

3. *Database designers need different information than application programmers.* Process modeling does an admirable job of conveying to system designers what the computer programs must do. However, it does a less effective job of conveying to database designers what the database must do. The process model conveys information about the changes data must undergo, such as "suspend customers." Data designers, on the other hand, need information about the relationships between data objects (e.g., a customer can have multiple addresses) and how a change to one object might affect other objects (e.g., when a customer is deleted, the address of the customer must also be deleted).

4. *Data requires a data-oriented, not process-oriented, method of documentation.* Although process modeling effectively describes real-world processes, it does not succeed in describing real-world data. Using a set of graphic and textual conventions, such as data flow diagrams and structure charts, process modeling techniques express the richness of process dynamics. However, these techniques do not ade-

quately describe the richness of the data. Data needs a modeling approach that will emphasize its focus and characteristics (Table 1.1). Information specific to data includes who creates it, what it looks like, how long it should exist, and how it changes over time.

Why Data Modeling Is Needed

Data modeling is one of the two major components of system development (Fig. 1.2). The other, described above, is process modeling. Why is data modeling needed? The main reason is that systems developers are so bad at building files and databases. Perhaps that is an exaggeration, but it is true that developers look to techniques such as data modeling to enhance less-than-perfect application development abilities.

In addition, development organizations are under increasing pressure to integrate applications, but attempts at integration through application code have proved to be slow, expensive, and overly complex. Since integration through data has been more successful, the need for and importance of data modeling has grown significantly. Data can be the glue that ties together otherwise disparate applications. However, with data integration comes the burden of not only understanding the data needed for just one application, but also knowing how the application's data fit into the larger organization.

Developers model data to ensure that they understand:

- *The user's perspective of data.* Data modeling, like process modeling, makes the distinction between the logical concept of *what* the user wants and the physical concept of *how* the system should provide it. In modeling the data, the developer uses a standard approach to capture facts about information and to verify and communicate those facts to the necessary parties.

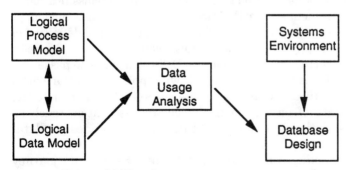

Figure 1.2   Data model life cycle.

- *The nature of the data itself, independent of physical representations or use.* By separating the logical from the physical, the essential and fundamental data definitions an organization needs are isolated from changes in

  Storage techniques.

  Data and file access methods.

  Specification of who uses the data and how it is used.

- *Its use across applications.* By keeping track of data definitions, life cycle information (who creates, updates, reads, and destroys data), and how and when data is used, data modeling makes integration across applications easier.

In fact, when properly applied, data modeling should catch and avoid a number of problems:

- *Duplication.* Data models help identify who uses the same data, when, and where. Application of this knowledge can ensure that the database does not mistakenly store the same information in multiple places.

- *Inflexibility.* By separating the definition of the data from its use, data modeling reduces the chance that small changes to data or processes will cause large and expensive changes in applications and databases.

- *Inconsistency.* Even without duplicate data, inconsistencies can occur (e.g., updating a customer's payment history without also updating the credit status). Data modeling permits the developer to modify one piece of data without the fear of contradicting another.

How Data Modeling Is Organized

In decades past, the phrase "data model" was used with modifiers such as hierarchical, network, or relational to describe a type or classification of a database management system (DBMS). More recently, "data modeling" has been used to refer to the process of specifying the logical definition of data rather than its physical characteristics. Using "data model" to refer to the physical structure of the data or the DBMS has become passé.

For purposes of this book, "data model" will apply to both the logical and physical structure of data, and "data modeling" will refer to the study of any state of data from its logical representation (such as through entity-relationship diagrams) through physical design (database schemata).

Since data modeling can represent data anywhere on its journey from the conceptual to a field in a program, it can best be described as a continuum with the ethereal and abstract at one end of the scale and the very concrete at the other end (Fig. 1.3). Any points in between are just that, points in between the start and end of a life cycle.

This is a somewhat more robust definition of data modeling than many people use. Analysts tend to concentrate on the logical aspects of data and, therefore, see data modeling as only logical. Database designers have a view of data at the more physical end of the spectrum. However, data modeling is, in reality, much more inclusive than either of those two perspectives, which is one reason why data modeling language tends to be confusing.

Logical data modeling

Data modeling is a technique that captures and communicates application development concerns to both technical and nontechnical users. In the first data modeling phase, logical data modeling, the data created or used by an organization is represented from the user perspective. The resulting model is

- End-user, not systems, oriented.
- DBMS or file system independent.
- Complete, containing a level of detail that serves as the input to the physical design process.

The logical data model is a major source of information for the physical database design process. For the system development life cycle phases after analysis, it provides the physical database designer with a vehicle for making the tradeoffs that are so important to an efficient database design. (Physical database design tradeoffs are discussed in Chap. 8).

But the logical data model also serves an important role after a project is complete. Properly maintained and kept up to date, the logical data model allows future changes to computer programs or data to be accurately and efficiently represented on the database. It also reduces or eliminates the need to recreate the logical data model every time an application is modified or a new one started.

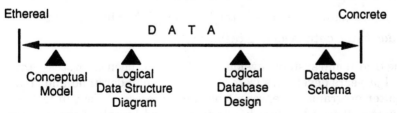

Figure 1.3 Data modeling continuum. Data modeling diagrams represent arbitrary points along a continuum.

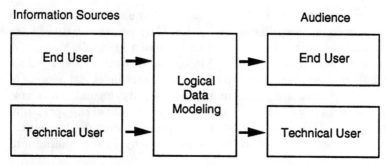

Figure 1.4 Data modeling sources and audience.

Physical database design

Physical database design, the second data modeling phase, is concerned with building physical or real information platforms (databases or files). It does this by taking the logical data model and the process model and turning them into instructions to create a physical database that will run in a specific systems environment. For example, a physical database designer might be charged with taking the logical data and process models for a payroll system and generating the computer commands to create a DB2 payroll database to store the payroll information in a manner consistent with its definition and use.

The physical database designer is, therefore, a user of the logical data model. The model becomes a communications tool that allows the designer to understand, in a standardized format, how end users see their data. In like manner, the process model tells the physical database designer how end users work with (process) their data (Fig. 1.4).

Common Obstacles to Modeling

In many organizations data modeling has not been very successful. Although the problems may vary from data processing shop to shop, a number of problems are common:

- Limited experience with the function, which
- Promotes confusion between the logical and the physical and
- Leads to the data modeling casualty.

The traditional system development focus has been on processes, not data. For years developers were taught how to understand and create computer programs to represent business processes. Few, in fact, are aware that their education has been confined to half of the development function.

Perform this test. Survey a group of system developers. Ask, "How many have had the equivalent of three college level courses in some type of process management (e.g., process modeling, program specification, coding). More than six related courses? Ten?" Then ask, "How many have had more than three courses focusing on data? Two? One?" If your sample group is close to the norm, most in the group will indicate they have had multiple college level courses in process-related matters but very few that focused on data. The fact is that data-oriented training is underemphasized in most schools and data processing organizations. The majority of data processors, unfortunately, have unwittingly become process zealots, and consequently their view of the data processing function often is misguided and their judgment in the development of applications clouded.

Broadly speaking, logical design is concerned with conceptual constructs, and physical design is involved with hardware, software, and the like (Table 1.2). While this is true, the concepts can be refined even further. Logical design (e.g., logical data modeling, logical process modeling) centers on *what* is needed, i.e., the statement of a problem. Physical design is concerned with *how* what is needed to solve a problem will be provided, i.e., the solution to the problem. Designers often confuse the two.

Logical design should be separated from physical design for three reasons:

- It deals with a different subject matter—the *what*, not the *how*.

- It is performed at a different time—the *what* must be understood before the *how* can be determined.

- It requires different skills, which are often found in different people.

Some people believe that the distinction between the *what* and the *how* is relevant, but that the distinction need not be taken too seriously. In other words, identifying both simultaneously is perfectly all right, and specifying physical database design options during logical

TABLE 1.2.   Logical vs. Physical Design Concerns

Logical Design	Physical Design
• What are the end user needs?	• How will the system deliver the required services?
• What do users want/expect?	• How should the hardware and software be configured?

data modeling is an acceptable practice. However, being guided by this perspective can lead to a serious problem, since the major cause of poor design is the lack of understanding of *what* is desired—not *how* to implement physical constructs.

The safest way to ensure that the physical design is complete and accurate is to guarantee that the problem, or the *what*, is completely and thoroughly understood. This will cause the "lowest common denominator" to surface and become the input to the physical design process.

Allowing logical designers to wander into physical solutions encourages them to shortcut the complete specification of the problem. When the problem is not completely understood, an acceptable and useful solution is doubtful, and a classic garbage in, garbage out (GIGO) situation is assured. For example, only through logical design can certain data concepts, such as exclusivity, modality, and multiple relationships between data objects (all of which will be discussed in later chapters), be adequately explored and consistently documented.

The goal of logical data modeling is not to ignore the solution but rather to completely and thoroughly understand and document the problem before becoming involved with the solution. Throughout this book this message will be reinforced. Remember:

First, completely and thoroughly specify what is needed. Then, and only then, examine how it can be implemented.

Overcoming the Obstacles

The solutions to the problems described above are education *and* experience. Knowledgeable developers correctly value the contributions of the various development components and, therefore, can make informed decisions. Logical data modeling, however, is a very subjective process. Give two experienced data modelers the same problem and the result might be two different data models. The issue is not that one is wrong, though this could certainly be the case, but rather that data modeling is an expressive skill that can result in different interpretations of the organization modeled.

The subjective nature of data modeling means that hard and fast rules, while helpful, will not give the data modeler all that is required. However, the experiences of others can aid the modeler. In the same way that a writer might study the works of Hemingway, or an artist the paintings of Chagall, data modelers can study and learn from the successes and failures of others—the best practices observed by experienced practitioners. Best practices are the experienced-based collection of rules, advice, and insight regarding the correct, most effective, and/or productive application of one or more techniques.

The guidelines included in this document are offered as a "starter set" of these rules. Alternatively, the guidelines can be used as the "straw men" to generate debate and a more appropriately customized set of rules. However, before entering the realm of components, rules, and guidelines, a clarification of the meaning of some of the data modeling terms is necessary.

The terminology trap

People often get caught up in the names and functions of different processes and diagrams, e.g., is it a conceptual model showing business data or a logical database with some DBMS information? The naming problem goes well beyond data modeling. In fact, information professionals have not been able to agree on the names or definitions of major information systems components for some time.

Take the systems development life cycle. Numerous interpretations and names exist for essentially the same functions (Table 1.3). What is the analysis portion of systems development called? General design? External design? Logical design? All of these terms have been used, and many more. And, except for some minor variations, they all describe the same basic activities.

Data modeling suffers from a similar though often more confusing problem. Different methodologies and approaches often refer to the same functions or diagrams by different names (e.g., conceptual model, enterprise model, business model, conceptual schema), and they use various names for diagrams representing slightly different locations along the continuum (e.g., logical database design, preliminary database design). Beyond these differences, data modeling phases do

TABLE 1.3.   System Development Life Cycle Terms

What the Project Is About	What It Should Do	How It Should Work	How to Build It

•Planning
•Requirements
  Definition
•Conceptual
  Design
	•Analysis
	•Logical Design
	•General Design
	•Systems
	  Analysis
	•Functional
	  Specifications
	•External Design
		•Design
		•Physical Design
		•Detailed Design
		•Systems
		  Specifications
		•Internal Design
			•Construction
			•Coding
			•Implementation

not always line up exactly with process modeling phases. This not only confuses data and process modelers and users but also creates a development cycle that produces deliverables at different and uncoordinated times.

Some authors use the term *logical database design* to identify the point between the most conceptual end-user data model and the physical database schema. The logical database design will have some physical characteristics but not all that are required for a physical database design. Usually the DBMS rules to be used are applied to the logical data objects, but not to storage or performance considerations. It is a sort of halfway stop between the conceptual and the physical.

Clearly, the term is confusing. Many analysts consider "logical" to mean relating to what the application is to do, not how it does it. As such, the choice of "logical" for this phase of data modeling contradicts the more general use of "logical" in process modeling. Likewise, logical database design does not coincide or align with a physical modeling process or system development life cycle phase. Rather it overlaps with the analysis and design phases. The result is that the process and data analysis phases end at different times and their deliverables will not always cover the same material (Fig. 1.5).

If you find the above confusing, you are not alone. The morass of names, phases, and deliverables has befuddled many a good system developer.

What the Project Is About	What It Should Do	How It Should Work	How to Build It
• Conceptual Model • Business Model • Enterprise Model	• Enterprise Model • Data Model	• Database Design • Database Schema • Physical Database Design	• DDL • Database Schema • Physical Database Design

• Logical Database Design
• Preliminary Database Design
(These functions cut across both the 'What It Should Do' and 'How It Should Work' phases)

Figure 1.5 Names of data modeling deliverables and phases.

Since the goal of data modeling is to increase communication and not confusion, terms such as "logical database design" will not be used in this book. Rather, terms will be used that are as consistent as possible across the process and data modeling spectrums.

A frame of reference

Before continuing, let's review the most frequently used terminology presented in this book. (For further reference, a complete list of terms is provided in the Glossary.)

A *model* is an abstract representation of a subject that looks and/or behaves, in one or more ways, like all or part of the original.

A *data model* represents the definition, characterization, and relationships of data in a given environment.

A *logical data model* is a data model of the information used in an organization from an end-user perspective, without regard to its functional or physical aspects. Although its meaning is more specific than the generic "data model," the two terms are sometimes used interchangeably.

A *physical database design (model)* is a data model configured to reflect the usage of data in a particular physical environment.

A *logical design* represents all the phases that identify the subject from the user perspective. This includes such traditional phases as planning, requirements, definition, and analysis.

A *physical design* represents the phases where the user's view of the application is turned into technical design specifications (Table 1.4). This includes such phases as detailed design and system specification.

The *user* is the beneficiary of a service.

TABLE 1.4.   Comparable Design Phases

Logical Design	Physical Design
• Planning • Requirements Definition • Conceptual Design • Analysis • General Design • Systems Analysis • Functional Specifications • External Design	• Design • Detailed Design • Systems Specifications • Internal Design • Construction • Coding • Implementation

End users are those who commission the building of an information system or will use the system commissioned. They are usually nontechnical staff, unless, for example, the system is an application tracking system designed to serve technical staff.

Technical users are system designers who use the output of other system designers. For example, designers write programming specifications for programmers, who are the designers' technical users.

Note: When modeling a publishing system, for example, a logical data modeler has two sets of users: the editorial staff, who represents end users, and the physical designers and programmers, who are technical users.

Organization and *business* refer to both the end-user organization and the ultimate recipient or client of a system. The terms will be used interchangeably and will refer to all types of end-user enterprises regardless of their purpose (e.g., commercial enterprise, government agency, not-for-profit organization, etc.).

A *technique* is a series of steps applied to a subject to change its representation. Data modeling, process modeling, and prototyping are all techniques.

A *tool* is a physical or conceptual construct that assists in the application of techniques. CASE products and flow charting templates are tools.

A *methodology* is the approach used to apply one or more techniques (Fig. 1.6). An organization might develop its own methodology or it might purchase one. STRADIS, Information Engineering Methodol-

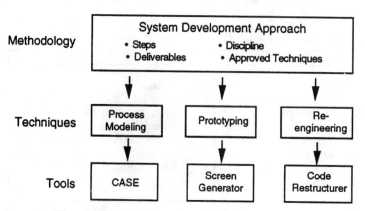

Figure 1.6 The relationships between methodologies, techniques, and tools.

ogy (IEM), and PROplanner are examples of methodologies that can be purchased. A methodology usually includes

Sequential steps to be performed.

Deliverables to be produced.

Discipline to be followed.

Project management techniques to be executed.

Doing the Right Thing

One of the difficulties that modelers face is knowing when they are doing the right thing. Since logical data modeling is to some extent subjective in nature, even determining whether information is relevant or properly presented can be a formidable challenge. Clearly, what is needed is a set of criteria to use in determining the appropriateness of logical data modeling decisions.

In the chapter that follows, the three underlying principles that form the basis of, or justification for, the data modeling function are discussed. Adherence to these principles increases the likelihood of success for the development project—and the developer.

2

Underlying Principles

*"Golden rule principles are just as necessary
for operating a business profitably as are
trucks, typewriters, or twine."*
JAMES CASH PENNEY

*"Great ideas need landing gear as well
as wings."* C. D. JACKSON

A common belief is that a system cannot be properly designed without the use of sophisticated development aids such as methodologies, techniques, or tools. This is simply not true. Some systems in place today, many implemented in the past decade, and most before that, were successfully developed and put into production without the use of development aids.

Of course, some may argue that systems were simpler in days gone by, and this is certainly true. But that is not the issue. Regardless of the degree of difficulty of a project or, for that matter, the tools and techniques available, good design and successful system development result from following a few simple steps. Everything else that supports system development is designed purely to help make the steps easier, quicker and less risky to execute. These steps, which do not change, are the:

- Determination of the problem to be solved
- Specification of a solution
- Construction of the system
- Implementation

As noted in Chap. 1, the major cause of system development failure is the inability of the designer to fulfill the first requirement, i.e., to completely, accurately, and intelligently identify the problem so that an appropriate solution can be developed. Created to help developers complete the first step, logical data modeling presents a clear picture of the data an organization uses without regard to functional or physical design constructs. The picture the model portrays is the information structure from the end-user perspective. It is the specification of what the system should represent and, therefore, a statement of the problem for which the physical designers must develop a solution.

Three overriding principles drive successful approaches to logical data modeling, namely, *communication, granularity*, and *logical representation*. Best practices need an empirical as well as a theoretical foundation. These logical data modeling principles are that foundation. Each is described below in detail.

The Communication Principle

Foster communication of business requirements to technical staff and end users alike.   Requirements must be clearly stated and understandable by all audiences, end-user oriented and consisting of detail that illuminates.

The major purpose of logical data modeling is to communicate the end-user view of the organization's data to those who will design the system. But the communication principle is not confined to end users. Many people of differing backgrounds and skills need to understand the logical data model (Table 2.1).

TABLE 2.1.   Groups Who Need to Understand the Model

Group	Need to:
• End users	• Affirm or correct the data represented on the logical data models
• Systems analysts	• Understand the data used in the logical process models
• Database administrators (DBA) and physical database designers	• Understand how the end user sees data so that the views can be accurately represented in the database design
• Analysts working on other projects	• See how this project defines data so that interfaces can be developed and data shared across applications

To facilitate communication with all these people, we will see that two separate logical data models are required: the business staff–oriented, end-user data model and the more technical detailed data model. The end-user data model, however, provides the most common view in the sense that even the detailed data model must support the end-user perspective of the organization's information.

When developing the logical data model documents and diagrams, the goal must be clarity. The intention is to communicate, not fog or confuse the reader in a tangle of technical gobbledygook. When adding data to the model, the modeler must ask, "Is this information adding to our understanding of the model or subtracting from it?" This does not mean that the model should not be, or need not be, detailed, but rather that what is needed is detail that illuminates, not clouds.

The Granularity Principle

Represent a low granularity of data and present a "lowest common denominator" of the structure of the information that the organization uses. Complicated structures should be broken down into their elementary parts, and unnecessary structure and duplication removed.

There is a misconception by some that logical design need not go into too much detail. Rather, the detailed look at the application can wait for physical design. This is not only a wrong position to take but a dangerous one to hold.

The granularity principle states that data should be as detailed as necessary to understand its nature and potential use. In fact, good and successful design dictates that the level of detail for the analysis phase be every bit as detailed as that undertaken by any other phase, including physical design. And if you think about it, it stands to reason that the specification of the problem has to be at a similar level of detail as the statement of the solution.

The logical and physical design processes fit hand in glove. Logical design breaks down a problem into its lowest logical components so that physical designers can build it back up into a physical interpretation of the logical problem. To do this, the level of detail of logical design must be at least as low as, if not lower than, the level of detail in the physical design (Fig. 2.1).

The problem many modelers encounter stems from a belief that the movement from the logical to the physical is one of decomposition. Nothing is further from the truth. The movement from logical to physical is not a decomposition but rather a transformation occurring at a common level of detail (Fig. 2.2). Like physicists who study subatomic

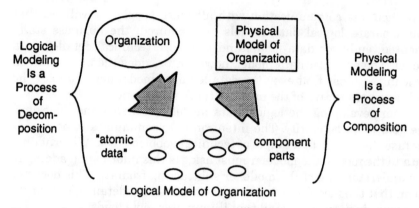

Figure 2.1 Logical design level of detail. Logical design breaks complex objects into their component parts—physical design reassembles them according to physical constraints.

particles, data modelers are after the elementary particles of the organization—atomic data.

All decomposition takes place during logical design. After the logical model is completely decomposed, the physical design process can begin. Physical design will "compose" a new physical model.

The Logical Representation Principle

Present a logical view of the organization's data.   The model should reflect a business orientation without physical constraints. Physical design options should be left open. The logical data model should not be tied to a particular architecture, technology, or product.

Lack of understanding is the major complaint end users have about system developers. And the users are probably right. However, more

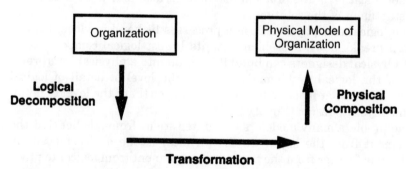

Figure 2.2 Moving from logical to physical design. Data modeling is a transformation process.

importantly, projects that are not grounded in what the user wants are suspect—and likely to fail. Consultants have become rich replacing in-house developers who have not adequately, or to user satisfaction, documented the application.

One of the major causes of poor documentation of existing applications is the propensity of analysts to jump into the physical design stage, i.e., the solution, prematurely. Generally, this occurs for one of two reasons, namely, to

- Cut corners because the outcome of a complete analysis is already known.
- Experience the excitement of coming up with the solution.

Unfortunately, confusing logical and physical design limits or misdirects the physical options that the project can pursue.

Cutting corners

Granted, some people just like to cut corners to make life easier. However, most analysts cut corners for the best of reasons, such as to avoid wasting time doing analysis that seems obvious or where the outcome is already determined. Let's take a look at a hypothetical situation to see how the story unfolds:

The Chicago Bean Curd Company (CBCC) is developing a new, state-of-the-art Bean Curd Production Control System, the heart of which will be a master database of temperature, mixture, and curing readings obtained from each vat every 5 minutes. In this way CBCC expects to provide an unprecedented amount of production control information to the automated and human quality controllers.

CBCC senior management, having recently attended a multimedia presentation at a DBMS vendor's headquarters, decided to use the VFRDB (Very Fast Relational Database) DBMS for the new production control system. Because they knew which DBMS they would be using, the logical data modelers decided to include a number of physical concepts such as foreign keys, which link related tables together, in their logical data model. This, they felt, would speed up the entire system development process.

Two problems occurred. First, when the CASE tool's relational database design program was executed, it automatically inserted foreign keys where it encountered a logical data model relationship, duplicating the foreign key fields already in the logical model. As a result, the designers had to manually go into each relational table and remove the duplicate entries and adjust table space sizes and free space allocations, costing the team a number of calendar days.

Second, the capacity planning group concluded that VFRDB DBMS could not accommodate the volume of data the application would generate. At least some of the tables had to be managed by some other, preferably nonrelational, DBMS. Now the designers had to go back to the logical data model and remove the relational specific information to generate a nonrelational schema.

Total cost to the project: two calendar months.

The problem at CBCC is rather common. In most cases, modelers are not able to know everything that can happen in the application development process, nor can they be absolutely positive about what is going to happen to the system in future decades. Consequently, the best course of action is to go "by the book" and document the problem in a way that is not solution-dependent.

Coming up with the solution

When investigating a problem, it is hard to put out of mind that flash of genius about how the database should be implemented. What should be done? Well, specifying a solution at this point is wrong because

- Not all the data is in, and the complete picture might dictate a different solution from the one conceived when only part of the problem was uncovered.

- Others reviewing the work will not be able to understand why the solution solves the problem, since the problem was not completely stated.

This does not mean that analysts should purge their minds of solutions. Good ideas are hard enough to come by without throwing them out. When a clever idea surfaces, it should be written down and passed along to the physical designers at the right time, which, you now realize, is after logical design.

Sometimes going back to logical design from physical design is unavoidable, as in cases where a logical design component is incorrect or was left out. Also, the "do logical first" tenet can seem to conflict with many new system development approaches, particularly those involving iterative steps of logical and physical design as in prototyping and rapid systems development (Fig. 2.3). However, even in situations where physical design constraints are dictated, logical design should proceed as if no constraints exist. Nevertheless, these cases do not change the logical representation principle. Whether logical design is a single 2-year phase, or many 2-week iterations, the principle is the same—understand the problem before specifying a solution.

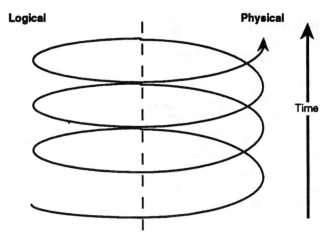

Figure 2.3 The application development process. Sometimes development involves going back and forth between logical and physical design steps.

One final observation. Separating logical and physical design helps partition the issues by skill, so that the right people are making the appropriate decisions—business analysts decide business issues, and technical analysts decide technical issues (not the reverse). The specification of the business problem should stand alone so that the physical designer's sole source of business input is the specification of the problem as documented in the logical design phase (Fig. 2.4). Executed correctly, physical designers will not have to go back to the users for additional information. If a physical designer has to go back to the user, the implication is that either the logical model was incomplete, incorrect, or both.

Using the Principles

The three principles—communication, granularity, and logical representation—are the cornerstones of modeling, be it data or process modeling, and should never be broken. They form the goals or, more

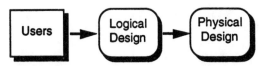

Figure 2.4 Separating logical and physical design.

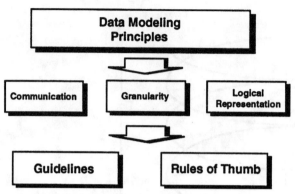

Figure 2.5 Principles as the cornerstones of modeling.

precisely, the reason for data modeling. Everything that is done, modeling-wise, should be to support one or more of these three tenets.

The logical data modeling guidelines and rules of thumb, presented in Chaps. 6 and 7, all are founded on these three underlying principles (Fig. 2.5). But before that discussion takes place, a firm understanding of the concepts and conventions of logical data modeling is required.

3

Reviewing the Basics

*"Though this be madness, yet there
is method in it."*   SHAKESPEARE

*"If people knew how hard I had to work
to gain my mastery, it wouldn't seem
wonderful at all."*   MICHELANGELO

A graphic-intensive technique, logical data modeling results in a data model representing the definition, characteristics, and relationships of data in a business, technical, or conceptual environment. Its purpose is to describe end-user data to systems and end-user staff alike.

Various methods of data modeling exist, which use a host of conventions and tools. The most popular approach, and the one this book focuses on, is called the *Entity-Relationship (E-R) Approach*, developed by Peter Chen in the late 1970s. Although E-R concepts have been modified and expanded by a number of authors and tool designers, most still have a strong Chen flavor.

With the introduction of CASE tools, the number of diagrammatic conventions that the data modeler will come across and must master has increased sharply. The characteristics of a number of tools are presented throughout this and the next chapter.

Data Modeling Objects

Entities, attributes, and relationships, the three types of data objects, are the basic building blocks of modeling:

- Entities are persons, places, or things about which an organization wishes to save information. Employees, States, Orders, and Time

Sheets are examples of entities. As a convention, the first letter of entities will be capitalized.

- Attributes are the properties of entities. Attribute examples include COLOR, NAME, EMPLOYMENT DATE, and SOCIAL SECURITY NUMBER. As a convention, attributes will be written in all upper case.

- Relationships are verbs that describe how entities relate to each other. For example, 'Customers *Buy* Products,' 'Employees *File* Time Sheets,' 'Sales Representatives *Place* Orders.' A sentence in this 'Entity Relationship Entity' construct is called a 'relationship entity pair,' which is a fashionable mechanism for representing many relationships. Relationship entity pairs are bi-directional. Thus, 'Customers Buy Products' is the same as 'Products Are Bought by Customers.' "Relationship" is meant to describe an end-user relationship, not some technical one. As a convention, relationship names will start with an uppercase letter, and relationship entity pairs will have initial capital letters and be in single quotes.

While a number of graphic conventions represent data objects, one convention that all the different approaches seem to agree on is the use of a rectangular box to represent an entity (Fig. 3.1). Relationships are represented by a line. Proper procedure is to label all relationships in both directions (Fig. 3.2). However, for various reasons, starting with time, space, and laziness, labeling relationships in both directions is often not done. One good reason is that it is often simply not needed if the meaning of the relationship is easily understandable.

Some modelers use a diamond to represent a relationship, with lines connecting the diamond and entity boxes (Fig. 3.3).

A special note. This book intentionally shifts back and forth between various diagramming techniques, thus forcing the reader to deal with different conventions. Hopefully, the exercise will be worth the inconvenience. An ideal approach, but one beyond the control of this book, is to set forth a single standard set of diagrammatic conventions. Alas, the ideal is, at best, years away. For the time being, serious analysts must learn to recognize a number of different graphic conventions.

Figure 3.1 Entity.

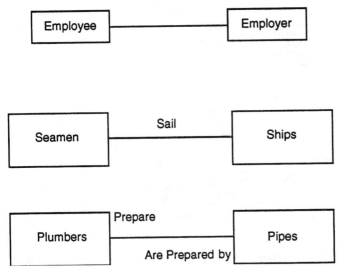

Figure 3.2 Relationship convention. Proper procedure is to label all relationships in both directions.

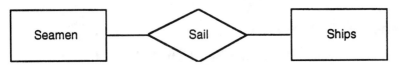

Figure 3.3 Alternative relationship convention.

Attributes are diagrammed in many different ways or not diagrammed at all. Some modelers place attributes in the entity box while others use ovals to hold attribute names (Fig. 3.4). However, most modelers do not place attributes on the diagram at all. They believe that diagramming attributes only makes sense for those simple models, presented in textbooks, which have perhaps a dozen attributes in total. In the real world, a diagram could quickly start to look like a Tokyo subway map as attributes are piled onto the page. A more practical approach is to keep attributes out of the data model and in the data dictionary, the repository of documentation about the data model.

A popular convention is to use the singular case for entity and relationship names, e.g., Customer and Product, and Files and Employs. Though this is a good idea, it is often not practical. Some entity names sound better when they are plural, as in Products or Students. Likewise, certain relationship names are better in the plural form, as

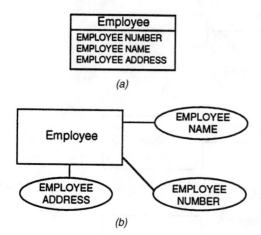

(a)

(b)

Figure 3.4 Diagramming attributes. (*a*) Some modelers place attributes in the entity box; (*b*) others place them in ovals.

"attend" in 'Students Attend School.' What is more important than a rule about the singular or plural representation is understanding, i.e., the representation of entity and relationship names must be understandable to the reader of the model. If that calls for plural entity or relationship names, then so be it.

Type/Occurrence Distinction

Before pressing on, the reader should understand the distinction between an entity type and an entity occurrence or instance. ("Occurrence" and "instance" will be used interchangeably.) An entity type represents the class of objects that share a distinguishing factor. An occurrence is a single case or instance of a type. For example, "Detective" is an entity type, while "Sherlock Holmes," "Hercule Poirot," and "Ellery Queen" are entity instances. The distinction between entity type and entity occurrence is the same as between record type and record occurrence. To say that entity type 'A' relates to entity type 'B' means that one or more occurrences of 'A' are (or can be) related to one or more occurrences of 'B.'

If this argument sounds familiar to you, it might be because you studied a similar issue in your college philosophy class. Philosophers have what they call the "type token distinction" where 'Man' can represent the set or 'type' of all men (and women—the ancient philosophers were rather chauvinistic) and 'Socrates' represents a single 'token' or occurrence of that set. Attributes and relationships, like entities, have types and occurrences. The distinction between type and occurrence is important for understanding the data modeling concepts of cardinality and modality, which are the two characteristics of relationships.

Membership Class (Connectivity Characteristics)

If entity 'A' relates to entity 'B,' knowing more about how the occurrences of 'A' relate to the occurrences of 'B' is important. One concern is the cardinality of the relationship.

Cardinality is the specification of the number of occurrences of one entity type that can be related to the number of occurrences of another entity type. Cardinality is usually expressed as simply 'one' or 'many.' For example, a husband can have only *one* wife (in most cultures), while a parent can have *many* children. Taking into consideration all combinations of 'one' and 'many,' two entities can be related as

- One-to-one (1:1)—An occurrence of entity 'A' can relate to one and only one occurrence of entity 'B,' and an occurrence of 'B' can relate to only one occurrence of 'A.' For example, a husband can have only one wife, and a wife only one husband (at least here in New Jersey).

- One-to-many (1:N)—One occurrence of entity 'A' can relate to one or many occurrences of entity 'B,' but an occurrence of 'B' can relate to only one occurrence of 'A.' For example, a mother can have many children, but a child can have only one mother.

- Many-to-many (M:N)—An occurrence of entity 'A' can relate to one or more occurrences of 'B,' while an occurrence of 'B' can relate to one or more occurrences of 'A.' For example, an uncle can have many nephews, while a nephew can have many uncles.

Note: The cardinality represents the maximum number of occurrences, not the minimum. An uncle could legitimately be related to only one instance of a nephew or even none.

The most popular way to represent cardinality—and to survive into the 1990s—is to use the "bar" to express 'one' and the "trident" (also called a "crow's foot" or "chicken foot") to express 'many' (Fig. 3.5). However, many other approaches exist (Fig. 3.6). Note that Chen and Reiner use a diamond to represent a relationship, while the trident approach uses just a line. The diamond, as will be seen later on, does a

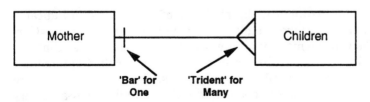

Figure 3.5 Cardinality.

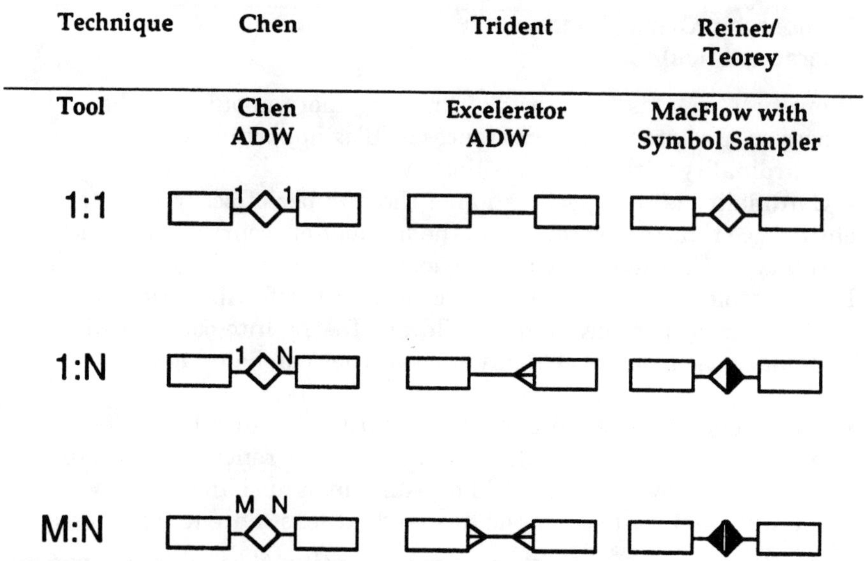

Technique	Chen	Trident	Reiner/ Teorey
Tool	Chen ADW	Excelerator ADW	MacFlow with Symbol Sampler

Figure 3.6 Diagramming conventions.

better job representing certain types of relationships but is not as good at showing the bidirectionality of relationships. Chen represents cardinality by using a '1,' 'N,' or 'M' on the relationship line (standing for "one," "many" and "many") while Reiner fills in the diamond.

Most tools now use the trident to show a cardinality of 'many,' while some give the user a choice of symbols.

The label "cardinality" is unfortunate. As used in data modeling, cardinality means either "one" or "many." The mathematical and more common definition of cardinality is a number such as 143 or 713. "Many" hardly qualifies as a number, which leaves us with "one" as the only real cardinal number used in data modeling, and even this has a historic glitch. The ancient Greeks believed that the first number was not "one" but "two," since you do not start counting things until you have more than one. Thus, if Aristotle was around today, he would say that the proper concept of cardinality is totally missing from data modeling, and where its use is attempted, it is misapplied.

In contrast to cardinality, the modality of a relationship indicates whether an entity occurrence must participate in a relationship. Cardinality tells you the maximum number of entity occurrences that can participate in a relationship, while modality (also called optionality) tells you the minimum number of occurrences. The modality values are 'zero' if an occurrence is not needed or optional, and 'one' if an entity occurrence is required or mandatory.

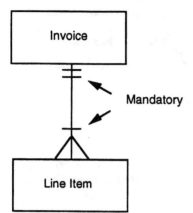

Figure 3.7 Mandatory relationship.

Let's take the example of Invoice and Line Item entities. An Invoice occurrence can relate to many Line Items, but a Line Item can relate to only one Invoice. This tells us the cardinality. However, is it possible to have a Line Item occurrence not related to an Invoice occurrence? The answer, of course, is "No." For a Line Item to exist, it must be linked to an Invoice. Therefore, the relationship is mandatory.

The same is true in the other direction. It makes no sense to have an Invoice without a Line Item. The relationship is mandatory in both directions (Fig. 3.7). A 'bar' represents a modality of one, a circle a modality of zero. The boxes in the exhibit below indicate where the cardinality and modality symbols are located on the relationship line (Fig. 3.8).

Let's look at the relationship entity pair, 'Artists Paint Pictures' (Fig. 3.9). Since it is not possible to have a picture without an artist, the relationship 'Pictures Are Painted by Artists' is mandatory. However, it is possible to have Artists who are not related to any Pictures (just go into Greenwich Village some Saturday night); therefore, in the other direction the relationship is optional. When dealing with the modality of a relationship, modelers usually refer to the one end of a one-to-many relationship first. This relationship, then, is mandatory-optional.

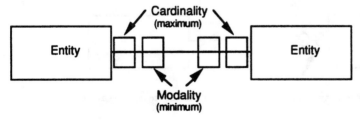

Figure 3.8 Cardinality/modality.

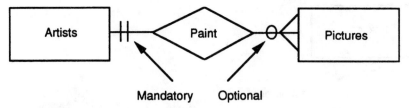

Figure 3.9 Mandatory-optional relationship.

The relationship 'Banks Finance Cars' is optional-optional, since you can have a bank that doesn't finance cars, and there are cars, I am told, which are not financed (Fig. 3.10).

Most data modelers use the term "optionality" instead of modality. This is an awkward and unfortunate use of the term because the optionality of a relationship could be either optional or mandatory. While an optional optionality appears redundant, it is not as bad as the seeming contradiction of a mandatory optionality.

Modality is a term taken from modal logic. It is used to distinguish necessary statements (whose truth is necessary or mandatory) from contingent statements (whose truth is conditional or dependent on external conditions). Modality is, in fact, a more accurate, meaningful, and less confusing term than optionality, and the one this book will use.

By now you have probably noticed that the 'bar' specifying a cardinality of 'one' can usually be inferred, i.e., since a cardinality of zero is not possible (Fig. 3.11), the bar is redundant (Fig. 3.12).

This is true, but the cardinality bar does serve a purpose. Since modelers do not always know the cardinality of a relationship, they must

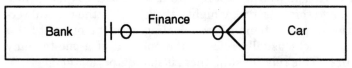

Figure 3.10 An optional-optional relationship.

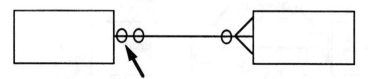

Figure 3.11 Cardinality cannot be zero. It is not possible to have a cardinality of zero.

Figure 3.12 Redundant cardinality bar. Some would say the bar is redundant.

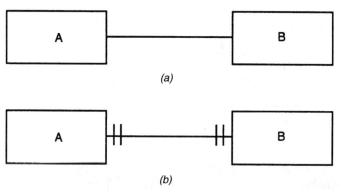

Figure 3.13 Distinguishing (a) "not knowing" from (b) a cardinality of "one."

have a way to distinguish 'not knowing' from 'one' (Fig. 3.13). In the latter case you know that 'A' and 'B' are related one-to-one; in the former you simply do not know, or have not chosen to show, the cardinality.

Note that many tool vendors do not require, nor do some allow, a bar for a cardinality of one. In that case, best practice is to specify the nature of the relationship in the relationship description.

Degree

Relationships can have any number of entity types associated with them. When an entity type is related to itself, the relationship degree is called unary or recursive (Fig. 3.14). For example, a child can be

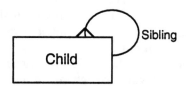

Figure 3.14 Unary relationship.

Figure 3.15 Binary relationship.

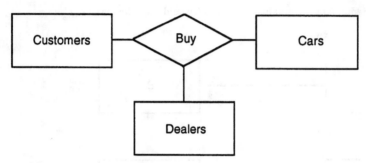

Figure 3.16 N-ary relationship.

related to another child through the relationship "Sibling." The most common relationship is the binary relationship which links two entity types. The relationship entity pair is an example of a binary relationship (Fig. 3.15). N-ary relationships are those involving more than two entity types such as 'Customer Buys a Car from a Dealer' (Fig. 3.16).

All data modeling tools support binary relationships, most support unary relationships, but only a few support n-ary relationships. The reason is that most database management systems only support binary relationships. This will be discussed in greater detail in another chapter.

Attribute Values

Like entities and relationships, there are attribute types and attribute occurrences. An attribute value is an instance or occurrence of an attribute type. An attribute value is a characteristic or fact about an entity occurrence. The fact might be that the entity's COLOR is "blue" (the convention will be to place attribute values in double quotes) or that the AUTHOR NAME is "Thomas Rowley."

Attribute values are what data processing is all about. They form the core of information management and represent the most tangible and least abstract aspects of all data processing.

Many data modelers divide the world into data and meta-data. Data consists of tangible data values such as "blue," "french fries," and "mustang." Meta-data is data about data. For example, the attribute type MENU ITEM tells us something about the attribute instance "curried pancakes," while the entity type Employee tells us something about the instances of employee. These objects are not "real data" but are used to describe the real data. They are called meta-data because they are one step removed from the data.

The word "meta" comes from the Greek and means "higher." Knowing a good thing when they saw it, philosophers quickly applied the word to most everything they did. The philosophical study of physics (reality) is metaphysics. The language used to study language is meta-language. And, of course, not to be tied too closely to the earth, philosophers even follow meta-ethics.

This sort of makes the meta-data-studying data modelers the philosophers of data processing—a conclusion most programmers would not challenge.

Domains

A domain is the set of possible values an attribute type can have. Examples of domains include dates, text, integers between 200 and 399, real numbers with two decimal places, state abbreviations (FL, NJ, . . .), etc. However, while "July 11, 1983" is an acceptable value for EMPLOYMENT DATE, "Curried Pancakes" is not.

Domains are important because they tell you not only what the acceptable values of an attribute are, but also how to use the attribute. For example, the following statement:

> MEDICAL COVERAGE = 'YES' if CLAIM DATE is
> greater than or equal to EMPLOYMENT DATE and
> less than or equal to TERMINATION DATE

only makes sense if the values for

- CLAIM DATE
- EMPLOYMENT DATE
- TERMINATION DATE

all share the same domain. If

- CLAIM DATE = "May 5, 1987"
- EMPLOYMENT DATE = "July 11, 1983"
- TERMINATION DATE = "123 South Main Street"

the results will be, as they say, unpredictable.

Domains can be very specific or quite generic. Generic domains such as 'integer,' 'text,' or the ever popular 'alphanumeric' (which excludes little), are the easiest to work with but also the least meaningful. Domains such as 'Dates between 1/1/50 and 12/31/94' or 'acceptable ZIP codes' are more useful.

Domains can also be nested, that is, the scope of one domain can incorporate another. The domain 'Dates between 1/1/50 and 12/31/94' is incorporated in the domain 'Dates' which is incorporated in the domain 'Integers,' and so on.

For purposes of understanding, one can speak of three types of domains:

- A *data type* is a programming language term that identifies broad domain categories, such as integers, real numbers, and text as well as the more specific dates, financial numbers, and U.S. dollars.

- *Ranges*, such as dates between 1/1/1950 and 12/31/1967, nonnegative values (e.g., real numbers between 0 and 4.0), and last names beginning A to J, indicate which values between two end points are acceptable.

- *Acceptable values*, e.g., ZIP codes, state names, and presidents of the United States, are the most specific types of domains. They specify the only values an attribute can have. Thus, the acceptable values for the GENDER attribute would be "Male" and "Female."

In effect, a domain hierarchy is created with the data type at the highest level and acceptable values at the lowest.

Just the Beginning

The E-R approach to logical data modeling does not end here. What has been set forth in this chapter is just a cursory view of some rather complex notions that are explored in detail in the next chapter. The road map in Fig. 3.17 highlights the topics already covered.

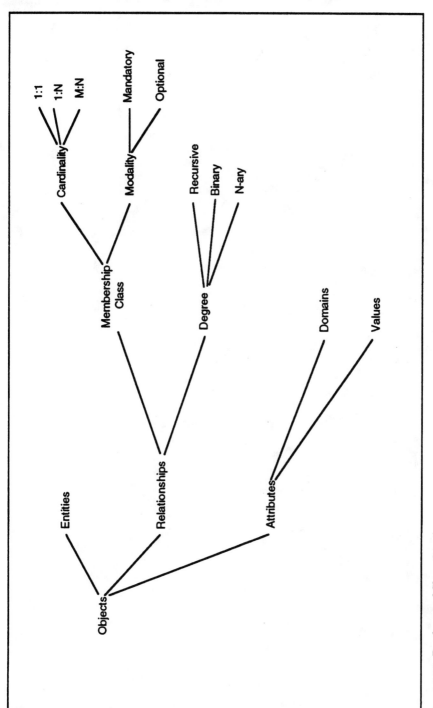

Figure 3.17 Road map of Chap. 3 topics.

41

4

More about the
Entity-Relationship Approach

*"What we don't understand we can
never possess."* GOETHE

*"If the only tool you have is a hammer,
you tend to see every problem as a nail."*
ABRAHAM MASLOW

No doubt, logical data modeling would be a relatively easy task if the building blocks described earlier could completely represent a business environment. Unfortunately, additional concepts are needed. This chapter will expand your entity relationship (E-R) tool kit with needed extensions.

- Ninety-nine percent of an organization's data can be represented with the techniques presented in Chaps. 3 and 4.

- The concepts that will be explored are the ones a modeler needs to understand to build logical data models.

- Many of the newer, more advanced E-R concepts are, for at least the next decade or so, beyond the ability of technology to deliver.

- Advanced E-R concepts are still developing and in a state of flux. Which will survive and how they will be used remains to be seen.

With that in mind, let us proceed to explore the depths of the E-R approach in more detail.

More about Entities

So far, the focus has been on standard, fundamental, or proper entities. However, there are other types of entities.

Associative entities

An associative entity represents a relationship that has attributes. Take the relationship entity pair, 'Customers Buy Cars.' The attributes DATE OF SALE and SALE AMOUNT are neither attributes of the entity 'Customers' nor the entity 'Cars,' but of the relationship 'Buy' (Fig. 4.1). When a relationship has attributes, it is called an associative entity and is "boxed" with an entity box (Fig. 4.2). The diamond in a box is a fairly universal way to represent an associative entity, even for tools that do not use a diamond to represent a relationship.

Attributive (weak) entities

An entity whose existence depends on another entity is called an attributive or weak entity (Fig. 4.3). Referring back to the example in Chap. 3, a Line Item entity is dependent on the Invoice entity, so it is

Figure 4.1   A relationship without attributes.

Figure 4.2   A relationship with attributes.

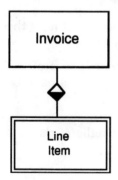

Figure 4.3   An attributive entity.

properly called an attributive entity. Some modeling approaches represent an attributive entity with a double box. Others use no distinctive graphic symbol.

Be careful not to confuse attributive entities with mandatory relationships. You can have one without the other, i.e., it is possible to have a mandatory relationship without entity dependence (Fig. 4.4). And it is also possible for an attributive entity to have an optional relationship (Fig. 4.5).

Note: Optional existence is "stronger" than entity weakness, since entities in an optional relationship with one entity can be in a mandatory relationship with another.

Subtypes and supertypes (generalization and specialization)

Subtypes and supertypes are best introduced with an example. Imagine a Customer entity that includes the attributes NAME, ADDRESS, CREDIT STATUS, and CUSTOMER TYPE (i.e., "Retail" or "Wholesale") (Fig. 4.6). However, the Customer entity also includes the attributes DISCOUNT, SALESMAN, and INDUSTRY CODE (which are only used if the customer is wholesale) and the attribute REFERRED BY (which is only used if the customer is retail). If half the customers are retail and half wholesale, then half of the time the attributes for DISCOUNT and REFERRED BY will be empty.

To resolve this situation, you could have two entities (Fig. 4.7), but this means that certain attributes, such as NAME, are repeated in

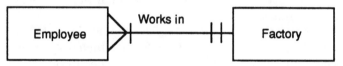

Figure 4.4 A mandatory relationship without entity dependence.

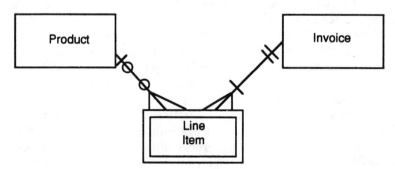

Figure 4.5 An attributive entity with an optional relationship.

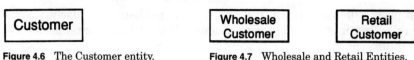

Figure 4.6   The Customer entity.

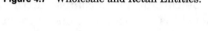

Figure 4.7   Wholesale and Retail Entities.

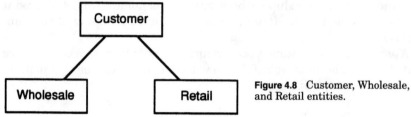

Figure 4.8   Customer, Wholesale, and Retail entities.

both entities—an ugly situation at best. Or you could create three entities—Customer, Retail, and Wholesale—where the common attributes are in Customer, retail-specific attributes in Retail, and wholesale-specific attributes in Wholesale (Fig. 4.8).

The three entity construct improves on the two entity construct, but it still hides important end-user information, namely, that Customer is a single business entity which plays two different roles—one as a wholesale customer and the other as a retail customer. This more robust view is substantially different from the construct of three separate entities and two relationships.

A better solution is the subtype/supertype construct. A subtype is a role an entity can play. The subtype contains the role-specific attributes and relationships. A supertype contains the common attributes and relationships of all the roles.

In the example above, Customer would be the supertype containing attributes such as NAME, ADDRESS, and so forth, which are common to all the subtypes. Wholesale and Retail would be the subtypes containing the attributes DISCOUNT and REFERRED BY, respectively.

Integral to the notion of subtype/supertype is the concept of inheritance. The subtype inherits from the supertype all the supertype's attributes and relationships. The subtype can have its own unique attributes and relationships in addition to those it inherits from the supertype.

Supertypes are represented any number of ways (Fig. 4.9). Unfortunately, most tools do not support these constructs, so they must be represented without any special symbols (Fig. 4.10).

When using tools that cannot differentiate subtypes and supertypes, note that the supertype and subtypes are linked in a one-to-one relationship and that each subtype occurrence must be linked to a supertype. The relationship is usually referred to by the clever name of 'Isa,' which stands for "is a," as in

- Employee *is a* Supervisor
- Employee *is a* Retiree
- Employee *is a* Trainee

A good idea, but the 'Isa' talk sometimes falls apart, as in 'Customer is a Retail.'

Bad as 'Isa' might be, sometimes it is the only way to communicate that what appears to be multiple entities and relationships is really a single entity with no relationships and many roles.

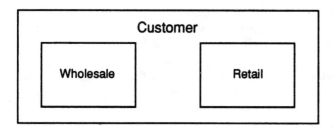

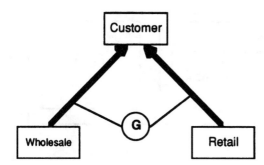

Figure 4.9 Examples of subtype/supertype diagramming.

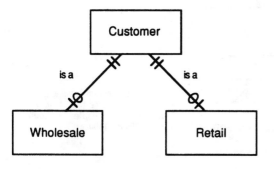

Figure 4.10 Subtype/supertype diagram without special symbols.

This notion of inheritance can go beyond just two levels, since a subtype/supertype structure can have any number of nested relationships (Fig. 4.11). All of these diagrammatic conventions work, but the boxed format has two advantages. It:

- Does not require phantom relationships.

- Can easily accommodate and represent n-level nesting.

So far, subtypes/supertypes have been used to distinguish common attributes found in the supertype from the specific attributes found in the subtype. However, subtypes/supertypes can also be used to distinguish generic from role-specific relationships. For example, the Wholesale and Retail subtypes for the entity Customer are appropriate, even if there are no role specific attributes, as long as the two subtypes have different relationships (Fig. 4.12).

The concept of an object inheriting common properties from its more generic parent has become the basis for the currently popular object-oriented design and programming techniques.

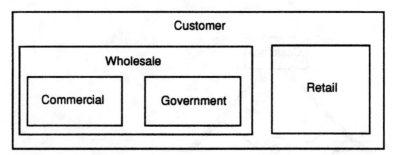

Figure 4.11 Nested subtypes.

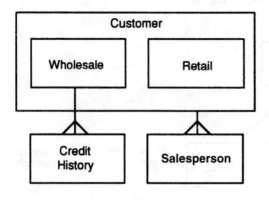

Figure 4.12 Generic and role-specific relationships. All customers are related to Salesperson, but only Wholesale Customers have a Credit History.

Subject areas

A subject area is a subset of a data model consisting of related entities. For example, the data model for a savings bank might include customer, account, and product subject areas, each containing a number of related entities.

Subject areas can serve a number of different purposes. First, a subject area can be the basis for dividing the data modeling workload among staff. If three teams will be developing a data model, assigning a separate subject area to each team reduces the interaction that must go on between teams.

Second, subject areas can be the basis for limiting the scope of a data modeling exercise. Referring to the above example, the exercise could be limited to just the customer entities.

Third, a subject area diagram could function as a very high level depiction of an organization's data (Fig. 4.13).

The first and second uses tend to have a top-down origin—the subject areas are developed first, and the entities are added later. The third use is more bottom-up and involves clustering existing entities by the subject they share. In either case, the result is an entity grouping or clustering based on commonality of definition.

More about Relationships

Relationship naming

The distinction between a relationship name and relationship label is perhaps a subtle one. A relationship name identifies a single relationship

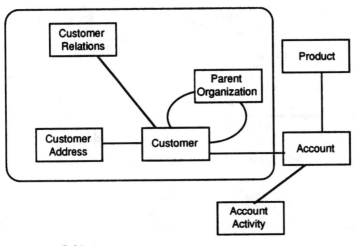

Figure 4.13 Subject area.

between two or more entities, such as the relationship 'Bake' in 'Bostonians Bake Beans.' A relationship label is what is written on the diagram.

With some diagramming techniques and tools, a single label is sufficient (Fig. 4.14). Others prefer a label in each direction (Fig 4.15). But both labeling techniques represent a single relationship.

By now you have probably figured out that the simple relationship entity pair, 'Customers Buy Products,' is rather arbitrary and could just as easily be written 'Products Are Bought by Customers' (Fig. 4.16). As stated above, many tools want you to name the relationship in each direction. Tool rules aside, labeling both directions is important if one label does not tell all. Otherwise, writing superfluous words on the chart can be confusing and messy.

Relationship constraints: Exclusion, inclusion, and conjunction

Relationships can also be linked to show that the occurrence of one relationship can affect the occurrence of another. This is called a *relationship constraint*. The three types of constraints are exclusion, inclusion, and conjunction.

Exclusion indicates that entity type 'A' can be related to entity type 'B' or to entity type 'C,' but not both. This is an *exclusive or* relationship. Note that this is not a single relationship, but two separate interrelated relationships. For example, either a Dealer or a Customer can own a Car, but not both. Reiner and Teorey represent exclusion with a very distinctive graphic (Fig. 4.17). Other authors represent exclusion

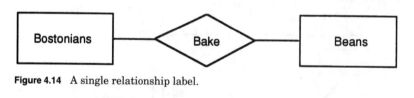

Figure 4.14   A single relationship label.

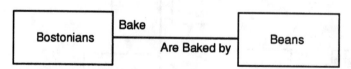

Figure 4.15   Labeling relationships in both directions.

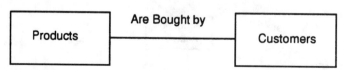

Figure 4.16   Labeling in only one direction.

using an arc (Fig. 4.18). Unfortunately, the majority of tools simply do not represent exclusion at all.

Inclusion, or an *inclusive or* relationship, is the easiest to understand and the most common. It indicates that 'A' can be related to 'B,' or to 'C,' or to both. If the above example were to be an inclusive or relationship, that would mean that the car could be owned by the Customer, or by the Dealer, or both. Obviously no special symbols are required.

Conjunction, or an *and* relationship, indicates that if 'A' is related to 'B,' it must also be related to 'C.' For example, a business might have a rule stipulating that if a customer has an outstanding balance, then the customer must have a payment plan (Fig. 4.19). Unfortunately, none of the tools presented in this book has a special symbol for conjunction.

Recursive relationships

Usually an entity occurrence of one entity type relates to an entity occurrence of a different entity type. When an entity occurrence is related to one or more entity occurrences of the same entity type, it is called a *recursive* or *unary relationship*. For example, if some employ-

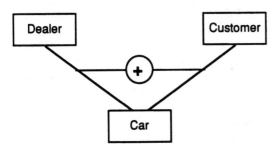

Figure 4.17   Reiner/Teorey representation of exclusion.

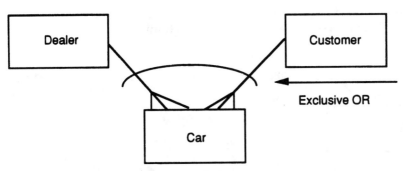

Figure 4.18   Using an arc to represent exclusion.

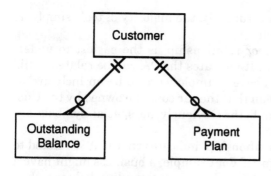

Figure 4.19 There are no diagramming conventions for conjunction. In this example, every Customer with an Outstanding Balance must have a Payment Plan.

ees supervise other employees, then the relationship, 'Supervises,' is from Employee to Employee (Fig. 4.20).

The recursive relationship is also useful for a hierarchy of unknown height. For example, if you know that an organization is divided into

- Region
- District
- Section

you can represent it as a three-level structure (Fig. 4.21).

However, suppose you do not know how many levels there are, or you know that regions are organized differently in different locations (i.e., some have districts and others do not). The recursive relationship lets you diagram a hierarchy of n levels (Fig. 4.22).

The recursive relationship is sometimes called the "bill of materials" structure, since it resembles a common parts problem. Imagine an auto parts data model. Since parts are made up of parts, which are made up of parts, etc., what would the structure look like? Using the recursive relationship, the model would create an n-level hierarchy.

Symmetrical and asymmetrical recursive relationships

A closer look at recursive relationships will show that there are really two different types. An example will be helpful.

Supervises

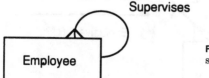

Figure 4.20 A recursive relationship.

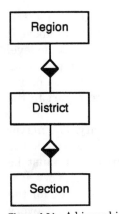

Figure 4.21 A hierarchical relationship.

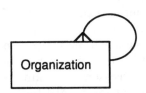

Figure 4.22 An *n*-level or recursive relationship structure.

Imagine a five-level organization having entities for International Headquarters, Division, Region, District, and Local offices (Fig. 4.23). However, what if all locations do not have all the levels? Let's assume that the Cleveland local office reports directly to the Mid-West region and not to a District office. And, in France some local offices have six or seven organizations between them and the Division level. This example is a classic case for an *n*-level recursive structure and can be represented with a recursive relationship.

Problems can arise, however, when you try to assign the modality of the relationship. There are four options: mandatory-mandatory, optional-optional, mandatory-optional, and optional-mandatory. Which is it?

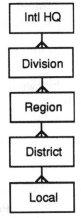

Figure 4.23 A five-level organization.

Some could argue that any mandatory relationship is impossible, for it would require that every occurrence have at least one level above it and at least one level below it. This is an infinite regress, since no level could be the top or the bottom. For example, the international headquarters occurrence would have to report to some organization occurrence, and some organization occurrence would have to report to the Cleveland local office.

Let's take another example—the Mayor entity for a city. The mayor can have a successor and/or be a successor (have a predecessor). Is the relationship 'Succeeds' mandatory or optional? Answer: It must be optional, for the first mayor had no predecessor and the very last mayor has no successor. (The same is at least temporarily true for the current mayor—at least until he has a successor.) To say that every mayor has a predecessor means that there must be an infinite number of mayors stretching back in time forever. Since this is impossible, the relationship must be optional (Fig. 4.24). This argument suggests that recursive relationships cannot be mandatory, but wait.

Now let's try a very different type of example. Let's say that the police department has a rule stating every police officer must have a partner and only one partner. This is a one-to-one recursive relationship that is clearly mandatory-mandatory (Fig. 4.25).

Here is another example. A dance contest requires that every dancer must have one and only one partner. Clearly, this relationship is also mandatory-mandatory (Fig. 4.26).

You can also construct mandatory recursive many-to-many relationships. The example below describes a relationship in which everybody (parent, sibling, cousin, uncle, etc.) relates to at least one other person and probably more (actually, at least two, since everyone has two parents). This relationship is clearly mandatory (Fig. 4.27).

What does all this mean? Why is it that in some cases it seems that mandatory relationships are impossible and in other cases possible? The answer is that there are actually two very different types of recursive relationships.

Look at the relationships in the two different situations. The cases where a mandatory relationship appears impossible are those with

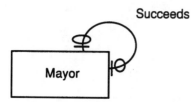

Figure 4.24 An optional-optional relationship.

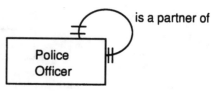

Figure 4.25 A mandatory-mandatory recursive relationship.

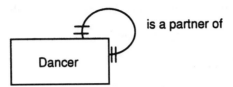

is a partner of

Figure 4.26 A mandatory-mandatory recursive relationship.

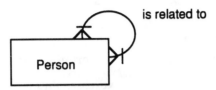

is related to

Figure 4.27 A mandatory many-to-many recursive relationship.

relationships such as 'Reports To,' or 'Succeeds.' The cases where a mandatory relationship appears possible are those with relationships such as 'Is The Partner Of' or 'Dances With.'

The first examples define a relationship that is asymmetrical, i.e., 'A' is related in some way to 'B,' but 'B' is not related in the same way to 'A.' Examples of asymmetrical relationships are 'Owns' and 'Hits,' since 'A Owns B' does not automatically mean that 'B Owns A.' Again, to say 'A Hit B' does not mean that 'B Hit A.' In this book, an asymmetrical relationship will be represented by a dashed relationship line (Fig. 4.28). (There is no standard for representing asymmetrical or symmetrical relationships.)

The second class of relationships is symmetrical. If 'A Dances with B,' then 'B Dances with A'; if 'A Is the Partner of B,' then 'B Is the Partner of A.' A symmetrical relationship will be represented by a double relationship line (Fig. 4.29).

Asymmetrical relationships are unidirectional implying a sequence or hierarchy that must have a beginning or end. Symmetrical relationships are bi-directional and have no beginning or end. Therefore,

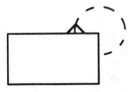

Figure 4.28 An asymmetrical recursive relationship.

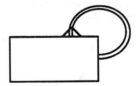

Figure 4.29 A symmetrical recursive relationship.

asymmetrical relationships cannot be mandatory, while symmetrical relationships can be.

More about Attributes

Attribute values

As mentioned earlier, an attribute value is the name given to an attribute instance or occurrence of an attribute type. A value is a characteristic or fact about an entity occurrence.

Primitive and derived attributes

The two different kinds of attributes are primitive and derived:

- A primitive attribute is one that expresses an atomic or nondecomposable fact (value) about the entity, as in the COLOR is "blue."

- A derived attribute is calculated from one or more atomic facts (values), or other derived attributes, by the application of an algorithm. For example, in the accounts payable system shown in Table 4.1, INVOICE AMOUNT is derived, since it can be calculated by adding up the ITEM AMOUNT values.

Primitive attribute information is placed in the data dictionary and the attribute assigned to an entity on the data model diagram. Derived data is placed in the data dictionary but is not usually assigned to an

TABLE 4.1   Derived Data.

Invoice

INVOICE NUMBER	DATE	INVOICE AMOUNT
12345	11/14/92	$ 150.79
23456	12/01/92	$ 839.77
54378	12/07/92	$ 43.43

Line Item

INVOICE NUMBER	PRODUCT	QUANTITY	ITEM AMOUNT
12345	Q12	1	$ 12.34
12345	L231	1	$ 23.32
12345	W13	1	$ 74.13
12345	AA7	1	$ 41.00

entity or placed on the data model. This is because, needing an algorithm to define its structure, derived data is closer to a process than to a data object. As such, process modeling techniques are better able to define its nature. (This topic will be discussed in greater detail in Chap. 6.)

Descriptors and identifiers

Descriptors and identifiers are two kinds of primitive attributes:

- Descriptors specify a nonunique characteristic of an entity or relationship (associative entity) instance. They are the standard, garden variety attribute, e.g., COLOR = "blue."

- Identifiers are also attributes, but they uniquely determine an entity or relationship instance, e.g., SOCIAL SECURITY NUMBER = "090-45-7894."

Many authors insist that all entities have an identifier, and some go as far as to say that there is one and only one primary identifier and any number of secondary identifiers—an obviously short jump to the physical design concepts of primary and secondary keys.

Identifiers and descriptors are important, but their real value is during physical database design, when primary and secondary keys need to be specified, not during logical analysis. If you know and can specify an identifier, do so, since it will make work down the road easier. But do not confuse their identification with logical data modeling requirements.

Compound identifiers

An identifier need not be confined to a single attribute. It can, in fact, be a group of attributes called a compound identifier. To illustrate the point, the attributes ACCOUNT NUMBER and DATE may both be required to identify an interest payment to a bank account. Leaving one of these attributes out would make the identifier nonunique. If there was a chance that two interest payments could be posted to the same account on the same day, then another attribute, such as TIME, would have to be added to the compound identifier. However, including multiple unique identifiers in the compound identifier, e.g., including both a SOCIAL SECURITY and EMPLOYEE NUMBER, is not necessary or recommended. If both are individually unique, then each is an identifier in its own right.

Multivalued attributes

Multivalued attributes describe cases in which an entity has an attribute with more than one value. For example, a customer might have multiple addresses; one for shipping, a second for billing, and a third for inquiries. Multivalued attributes should not be modeled. Rather, they should be treated as a single value and placed in their own entity in a one-to-many relationship with their parent. In the case of a customer with three addresses, the addresses will form a new attributive entity (Fig. 4.30). Then, an attribute such as ADDRESS TYPE in Address would identify the kind of address occurrence, i.e., "shipping," "billing," or "inquiry."

And What about Normalization?

Let's start off by saying that normalization is not part of logical data modeling. However, given a persistent belief that it is and that it should be performed and completed during data modeling, the logical data modeler cannot ignore it.

Normalization is a physical database design technique that involves applying a set of mathematical rules to the data model to identify and reduce insertion, update or deletion (IUD) anomalies. It comes from relational theory where data is represented as a series of two dimensional arrays or tables. A method was needed to transform more complex data into the simpler relational format. Normalization provided the solution.

An IUD anomaly is a data integrity problem that occurs in one area of a database when an insert, update or delete occurs in another. For example, let's take a Scotland Yard Case Time Reporting System represented in Table 4.2.

This table suffers from IUD anomalies. First, we cannot insert a new case until it is assigned to an inspector. This is called an insertion anomaly. Second, if we discover that Inspector Lestrade spells his name 'Lestrede,' we must change every Lestrade record. This is called an *update anomaly*. Last, if Inspector Gregson quits the force and we delete his records, we lose information on how many hours were applied to the different cases. This is a deletion anomaly.

To remove the anomalies, the time sheet table must be broken up. We can do this in two ways. We can think of every possible way we will

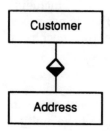

Figure 4.30 A multivalued attribute as a new entity.

TABLE 4.2   An Un-normalized Table: Scotland Yard Time Sheet File

Inspector	Date	Case	Hours on Case
Lestrade	1887	Empty House	120
Lestrade	1872	Six Napoleons	342
Lestrade	1892	Second Stain	456
Lestrade	1890	Cardboard Box	12
Gregson	1896	Silver Blaze	760
Gregson	1895	Red Circle	123
Hopkins	1897	Abbey Grange	45

NOTE: The underscore denotes the key (identifier) of the file (entity).

need to understand the data stored in the table, a daunting task; or we can apply the rules of normalization.

Normalization is expressed in levels, with first normal form (abbreviated 1NF) being the lowest level, 2NF higher, etc.:

- First normal form requires two conditions: first, every record must have a primary key that uniquely identifies the record; and, second, no record should contain any repeating groups. If a record meets these two conditions, then it is in first normal form. (*Note*: The above referred to "records" and "fields" and not entities and attributes. This was done to emphasize the fact that normalization was developed as a physical database design technique, not a logical data modeling one.)

- To be in second normal form, a record type must be in 1NF and every nonprimary key field in the record must be dependent on the entire primary key for its existence. If the primary key is compound (consisting of multiple fields), then each nonkey field must be dependent on all the fields of the key, not just part of them.

- To be in third normal form, a record must be in 2NF and the nonkey fields must only be dependent on the primary key for their existence, not on any other field.

The highest level is somewhat uncertain. As with subatomic particles, some academic is always coming up with a new record. By last count, researchers have uncovered seven levels. However, those in the know agree that, for most situations, 3NF is as high as one need go.

The process of normalization works by splitting offending record types. When a record type is felt wanting, it is split into two or more to achieve the desired normalization level. For example, if a record type has repeating groups, the groups are removed and placed in a new record type created for the repeating elements only. If second normal form is not achieved, then the elements that are dependent on the partial key are stripped out from the record type, and, with the partial key, a new record type established which meets the 2NF criteria. As you can see, normalization is a reduction process of removing offending elements and placing them in new record types until the desired result is achieved.

Normalization is a valuable addition to data modeling. Though in concept a physical design process, it can be applied successfully to logical data modeling in certain circumstances. Whatever amount of normalization that can be completed in logical data modeling should be undertaken. However, normalization requires a number of concepts (specifically, the designation of primary keys) that will be missing from some logical data models. Since logical data modeling does not require primary keys, the data modeler must choose between either suspending further normalization until physical database design begins or "forcing" keys into the model. Data modeling best practices would strongly recommend the former, not the latter.

Logical data modeling and normalization should not be confused. Their purpose and function are quite different. While data modeling is a communications technique, normalization is a data integrity technique. Data modeling deals with the relationships between entities, while normalization is concerned with the relationships between attributes. For example, for a record to be in third normal form, all the nonkey fields should relate only to the key and not to any other fields. For data modeling, the only relationship an attribute can have is to describe an entity.

A Few Last Words

As mentioned earlier, the E-R approach to logical data modeling is quite rich and does not end here. The intent of these last two chapters is to offer the modeler a data modeling "starter set" (reflected in the data modeling organization chart in Fig. 4.31) incorporating what the in-the-field modeler *must* know.

New E-R techniques continue to emerge. To keep up with advances as they unfold, you may want to contact the Entity-Relationship Institute (E-RI), which is considered to be the best source of information on the subject. The E-RI has annual meetings, alternately held in North America and overseas. Since the membership is comprised of individuals in academia and industry (the ratio is about 50-50), the organization offers a well-balanced forum to meet member needs.

The next chapter describes the practical issues involved in building the logical data model, including interviewing users, verifying and maintaining the model, and the diagramming and conceptual conventions of a number of data modeling tools. Some data modeling do's and don'ts are also discussed.

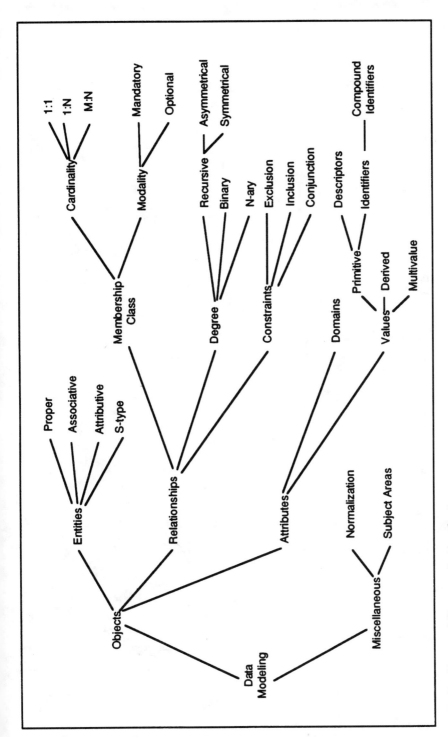

Figure 4.31 Data modeling organization chart.

5

Building the Logical Data Model

*"The method of enterprising is to plan with
audacity and execute with vigor: to sketch out
a map of possibilities, and then to treat them
as probabilities."*   BOVEE

*"When we mean to build,
We first survey the plot,
then draw the model."*   SHAKESPEARE

The truth is that building a logical data model is a rather simple process. You just need to follow the steps presented in this chapter and you will have a data model.

Whereas the process is simple, it is not easy. In most cases, you have to interact with other people to data model—and people complicate things. Granted, they may have a common goal, but that neither implies they have a common agenda nor a common path to that goal. And so, contrary to what the pundits profess, getting there is often not half the fun.

However, this does not mean that all is hopeless. There are steps one can take to ease the transition from here to there. What follows lays the foundation for how to build, verify, and maintain a logical data model—without going crazy.

The Process

Logical data modeling is not just an exercise for technical staff. To be effective, users must be intimately involved, and the involvement should begin as early in the process as possible. Data modeling is an iterative process that has a starting point and an almost endless procession of refinements. The model is chiseled, crafted, and refined until it honestly and effectively represents the subject.

At its simplest level, logical data modeling is a series of rather non-imposing steps.

1. Identify users who are authorities or experts on the subject.
2. Meet with experts and identify the top 10 "things" (entities) the subject (application) is about.
3. Identify relationships between the entities.
4. Define in detail both the entities and their relationships.
5. Review, one at a time, each entity and relationship, expanding the model, as necessary, with new entities and relationships.
6. Identify the properties or attributes of entities and relationships.
7. Formalize definitions.
8. Review results with users.
9. Repeat steps 4 through 7 as necessary.

The process can begin as early as the initial requirements phase, or it can wait until the analysis phase. Additionally, it can be performed one on one or in a group setting.

As the first step, you must identify who must be consulted to understand the subject. The list can include end-user and technical staff and extend from senior management to junior clerks. You should be selective in your choice of interviewees and ensure that they represent all aspects of the business—include both those who are knowledgeable about the way things are and those who know the way they *should* be done. This last point is important. All too often a new system merely offers a faster, cheaper way of doing things the same way they have always been done, when what really is needed is a new way of doing things. So, talk to both the historian and the visionary, but remember which is which.

Since the interview list will probably include both end-user and technical staff, you can expect to encounter differences in the response to application development techniques such as data modeling:

- End-user staff

  Open to application development techniques, or
  Indifferent or hostile to the process

- Technical staff

  Technique literate—aware of techniques, if not knowledgeable, or
  Open to new techniques and ways of developing systems, or
  Hostile to techniques

Some people will be receptive to the process, but others will be openly hostile. Oddly enough, the hostility often comes from the technical rather than the business side. While some may genuinely question the validity or payback of the techniques, many more will feel threatened by them. New ways of doing things represent change, and change is often the most difficult thing for people to accept. The successful modeler will have to recognize and negotiate these hurdles.

No doubt, some people will be selected for interviews for political reasons. Usually they are too important or noisy to ignore. In these cases you should go through all the proper steps, but in the end use your judgment to decide what should be in the model and what should be excluded.

Though a certain amount of data can be gained from documents, most information will be gathered from personal interviews (if nothing else, the interviews can tell you what documents exist and which should be read). The two approaches for collecting data through interviews are the *informal one-on-one interview*, discussed below, and *facilitated joint sessions*, involving a number of participants.

Informal One-on-One Interviews

The most common way to gather data modeling information is the one-on-one interview. It involves sitting down with an interviewee and asking questions about the data related to the subject and/or the interviewee's expertise. Sessions are usually 45 minutes to no more than 3 hours, but often a number of return visits to resolve questions, confusions, and issues are necessary. A good way to get started is to ask the interviewee to name the 10 basic "things" with which the business is involved.

Examples are useful. You might start by suggesting common entities such as customers, accounts, or employees. When you have identified about 10 entities, start asking about the relationships between them, i.e., "Can a customer have more than one account?"

Some interviewees will be able to expound on their data, but most will need you to prompt them. (User soliloquies are more likely to occur during process modeling interviews, where a known sequence of steps or events exist; they are rare in data modeling.) You should be prepared to take the lead with a series of easily answered questions.

The information collected can be either written down in long hand or diagrammed on the spot, whichever method you prefer. If you are new to data modeling, you might not feel comfortable extemporaneously drawing diagrams. However, if you can diagram on the fly, do so because diagrams make it fairly easy to identify problems and omissions and can function as the trigger for your next question.

Unpacking a statement

Converting interviewee ramblings to data modeling input is a bit of an art, since it involves translating English to an E-R diagram. In Chaps. 3 and 4, you learned that if you are told that "Customers can have more than one account, but that an account can be for one and only one customer," you can easily convert the statement to an E-R diagram (Fig. 5.1). What you have done is convert the English parts of speech and text to data modeling objects and constructs. "Customers" and "accounts" become entities, "have" becomes the relationship "Owns," while the language "one and only one" becomes the cardinality and modality of the relationship.

Table 5.1 is a chart that is helpful when translating English into data modeling-ese.* To use the chart, you look up the English part of speech or the words used on the left side of the chart and read the data modeling construct on the right. Take the following example:

"Employees can report to either a supervisor or the personnel department."

- "Employee" and "Supervisor" are common nouns and, therefore, entities.
- Since "Personnel Department" is a proper noun, not a common noun (such as "organization" or "department"), you should create an entity called Organization with an occurrence containing the attribute data value, "Personnel Department."
- "Report" is a verb and, therefore, your relationship.
- Exclusion is implied by the words "either...or."
- "Can" indicates that the relationship is optional, but you already know that from the exclusion construct.
- The plural of "employees" and the singular form for "supervisor" and Organization tell you that the cardinality is one to many.

What the statement does not tell us, however, is the complete modality of the relationship (i.e., must a supervisor have at least one report?). Nor does

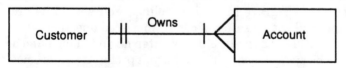

Figure 5.1 An E-R diagram expresses English statements.

---

*A more detailed account of converting English syntax to data modeling constructs can be found in Peter Chen's excellent paper on the subject. See Appendix C for details.

TABLE 5.1   English to E-R Conversion Chart

What to Look for	E-R Component
Common Noun	Proper Entity
Transitive Verb	Relationship
Gerund	Associative Entity
Adjective	Proper Entity Attribute
Adverb	Relationship Attribute (Associative Entity)
Words such as: "many" "at least" "one" "only one" "at most"	Cardinality
Words such as: "must" "can" "may not"	Modality
Words such as: "and" "but"	Conjunction
Words such as: "or" "either...or" "nor" "neither...nor"	Exclusion

it tell us if "supervisor" should be an entity or a role (subtype) of Employee (Fig. 5.2). These issues will have to be probed by the interviewer.

Let's take a second example:

"Orders are shipped from the warehouse promptly."

- "Orders" and "warehouse" are common nouns and, therefore, entities.
- "Shipped" is the verb and, therefore, the relationship.
- "Promptly" is an adverb, so it is a relationship attribute. (Actually, it represents two attributes—ORDER DATE and SHIPPING DATE—which means that "shipped" is really an associative entity (Fig. 5.3).)

But some statements are more difficult, and neither the English to E-R diagram technique, in particular, nor data modeling, in general, can accurately represent them. For example:

"An employee cannot report to his or her spouse."

"Employee" is an entity and "reports" a relationship. What might not be so obvious is the second relationship implied by the word "spouse." The diagram might look something like that in Fig. 5.4. What you cannot capture in the diagram is the fact that if the nature of the family relationship between two employees is 'spouse,' then one cannot report to the other.

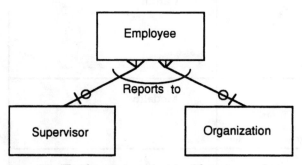

Figure 5.2 "Employees can report to either a supervisor or the personnel department."

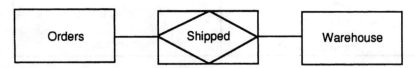

Figure 5.3 "Orders are shipped from the warehouse promptly."

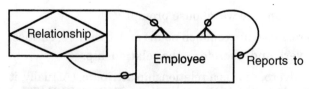

Figure 5.4 "An employee cannot report to his or her spouse."

There is an important lesson in this example. If data modeling models data, and process modeling models processes, which technique models rules? Actually, and unfortunately, the answer is both. Rules such as "Every employee is assigned to one, and only one, department" are easily modeled by E-R techniques. However, that an employee cannot report to his or her spouse cannot be modeled by current data modeling techniques alone. You must also use process modeling to represent rules.

It would be nice if there were some rule modeling technique that could be used to review all business rules. But for now, at least, to understand the rules of the business you must examine both the data and process models.

The two data modeling layers

So far, emphasis has been on how data objects are represented on a data modeling diagram, but this is only part of the story. In fact, a data model is both a:

- Graphic representation depicting some or all basic data objects—the data model diagrams, and a

- Repository of information about the data an organization uses or needs—a data dictionary.

You can, therefore, look upon a data model as consisting of two layers, the:

- Documentation, consisting of the data dictionary, and the

- Presentation, consisting of the diagrams.

The documentation layer contains all the data one needs to create the presentation layer, but not everything in the data dictionary is on the diagram. For example, as mentioned in Chap. 4, derived data is not included on the diagram, nor are the totals that appear on a report. This data will eventually need to be documented, but it would not be represented on the logical data model diagram.

Information required for data modeling

During the interview, you will have to collect rather detailed information about each of the data objects identified. As noted below, the information should include, but not necessarily be limited to, complete definitions of entities, relationships, attributes, and, for the attributes, domains.

1. Entity definition
    a. Name
    b. Description
    c. Entity type—proper, associative, attributive
    d. Synonyms or aliases (other names for this entity)
    e. Attributes in the entity
        (1) Name
        (2) Role—descriptor, identifier, part of a compound identifier
        (3) Occurrence type
            (*a*) 0–1   Zero or one occurrence possible
            (*b*) 1   One occurrence required
            (*c*) 0–N   Zero to N occurrences possible ($N>0$)
            (*d*) 1–N   One to N occurrences possible ($N>1$)
            (*e*) X   Exactly X occurrences required ($X>0$)
        (4) Percent of time attribute occurs
    f. Number of occurrences of entity
    g. Growth rate
    h. Insertion, Update, Deletion rules
    i. Notes, constraints, other rules, and comments
2. Relationship definition
    a. Name
    b. Description
    c. Relationship type
    d. Entities in relationship
    e. Cardinality
        (1) Minimum
        (2) Maximum
        (3) Average
    f. Modality
    g. Notes, constraints, rules, and comments
3. Attribute definition
    a. Name
    b. Description
    c. Synonyms or aliases (other names for this attribute)
    d. Attribute type (primitive, derived, etc.)
    e. Domain
    f. Size
    g. Notes, constraints, rules, and comments
4. Domain definition
    a. Name
    b. Description
    c. Length (minimum, maximum, average)
    d. Format
    e. Abbreviations

   f. Validation rules
   g. Default values
   h. Acceptable values
   i. Notes, constraints, rules, and comments

However, not all tools have dictionaries that can store all of this data. In those cases, you will have to find some other way to store the information.

One acceptable solution is to include the information in the data object comments field, which is found in most tools. For reporting purposes, you might want to develop a convention for identifying the information. To signal a special field within the comments area, for example, you could reserve words spelled in full caps, as in

DOMAIN = Dates between 1/1/50 and 12/31/99

In this example, full caps signals that the following information is the domain of an attribute.

Verifying the model

The two methods of model verification that should be used are immediate interview feedback and formal walk-throughs.

Clearly, the best time to correct mistakes and omissions is during the interview process. The recommended approach is to constantly read back to the interviewee what you heard. This not only ensures that you understand what was said, but also gives the individual an opportunity to correct what was said.

Remember: Since most nontechnical staff will understate business rules and constraints, you most likely will have to push them to understand the boundaries of entity relationships. For example, if you are told that every account is owned by a customer, you should follow up and ask whether or not firm, transient, suspense, or general ledger accounts exist. If you are told that there is only one customer for an account, you might ask if multiple family members can use the account. You have to probe to test the limits of what you are being told. This gets back to the emphasis on the question/answer approach to interviewing.

After you have added the input from other interviews and your own analysis to the data model, you will want to go back to some, or all, of those interviewed to show them a draft of the result for their comments, corrections, and additions. In contrast to immediate feedback, these formal walk-throughs generally take place some time after the initial interviews.

Since, to the interviewee, data modeling probably looks more confusing and less appealing than Chinese arithmetic (Fig. 5.5), you will have to "walk" or guide the user through the model. You have three choices:

"You users should review the data model and
get back to us tomorrow with any changes"

Figure 5.5 Verifying the model.

- Escort the interviewee through the data modeling diagram slowly and confirm each item.
- Convert the model back into English and read the model aloud in a narrative style.
- Do both.

Which method you choose will depend on the receptivity of the interviewee to data modeling mumbo jumbo.

With some interviewees you may be able to draw the model on paper or a white board during the initial interview or, alternatively, unveil the printed model during the walk-through. If you describe what you are doing line by line, many people will be able to follow the analysis sufficiently to point out errors and omissions. Other people are more comfortable being "read" to, in which case you should be prepared to interpret the data model to them in English.

In either case, keep the conversation on an end-user level. There is no better way to stop a promising interview or walk-through than to get into techno-babble. Talk about end-user data, end-user activities, and end-user relationships—not about entities, attributes, or cardinality.

Data modeling tools will be discussed later, but one point is appropriate here. By and large, tools have not changed the technique of data modeling. The thought process and interpersonal skills, which were required before tools existed, are still needed now. However, tools do allow the use of new views of the data that can facilitate user understanding. Two new and useful advances are the neighborhood diagram and the entity fragment.

Neighborhood diagram

For many projects the data model can grow to 200 or more entities and the same number of relationships. An imposing diagram. However, a number of tools allows the production of a neighborhood diagram, which shows one entity at a time with only its relationships and the entities that are also tied to those relationships. If the data model has 200 entities, then there are 200 neighborhood diagrams—but only those entities relevant to the interviewee need be examined during the walk-through. With neighborhood diagrams, many users, who are not candidates to see the complete data model, can review a graphic representation of their data without becoming overwhelmed (Fig. 5.6).

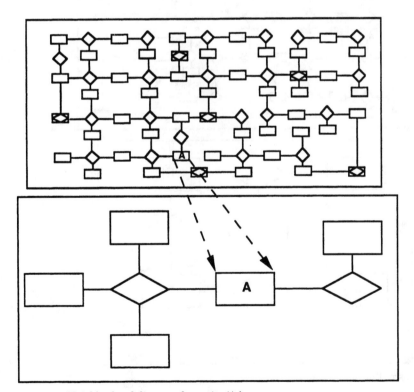

Figure 5.6 Neighborhood diagram for entity 'A.'

Entity fragments

An entity fragment is a view or portion of the data model that deals with a specific process. Take the example of the "Update Customer Account" function. This process might need Customer, Account, and Credit data, but might not be concerned with the Production Schedule, Raw Materials, or Distributors entities. Some tools allow modelers to create a subset of the data model specifying only the entities, attributes, and relationships relevant for a specific process. When reviewing the process, the entity fragment is displayed showing only process-relevant data (Fig. 5.7).

Data model acceptance

A constantly changing data model is not useful input to physical database design. A point has to be determined at which the modeling process shifts from development to maintenance. Acceptance indicates

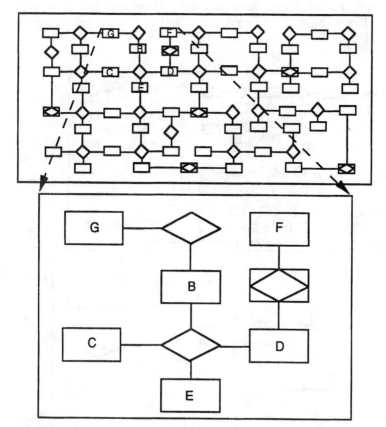

Figure 5.7 Entity fragment diagram.

that the model accurately reflects the business at a point in time. Subsequent changes will be handled through a change control process and possible follow-up interviews.

Acceptance is a rather formal process involving a representative of the business who states that the model is accurate, complete, and adequate as one of the design criteria for application development.

In practice, many users are reluctant to sign off on anything that doesn't produce something tangible, such as a functioning system. The modeler must explicitly describe what the user is getting into by "signing off" and what he or she is getting into by *not* "signing off." If clearly explained, the objective—that of gaining acceptance—usually results.

Facilitated Joint Sessions

The new alternative to the standard one-on-one interview is called the facilitated joint session. It differs from the one-on-one interview in a number of ways:

- A single session can last from 1 to 5 days.
- From 6 to 12 people can be involved.
- Very specific and defined roles are assigned.
- The session follows a formal set of rules.
- Follow-up sessions are rare.

There are various types of facilitated joint sessions, such as IBM's Joint Application Design (JAD) and Booz•Allen's Joint Enterprise Development Interviews (JEDI), but all share the common feature of being a workshop led by a facilitator who orchestrates and adjudicates the discussions—sort of a data modeling version of Phil Donahue. In addition to a facilitator, scribes record the proceedings and draw diagrams, and attendees contribute the information. Attendees are usually of two types: users who know the business, and systems staff who either know the workings of the current systems or are involved in the development of the new system.

Data modeling tools can be used during the session to quickly represent the current discussion. With PC projection equipment, the entire room can be viewing the model as it is changed to represent new information.

The goal of the session is to derive a complete data model in the few days allotted. The rules stipulate that everybody is to be present for the entire session, that all are heard, and that neither an individual nor an issue dominates the meeting. The result at the end of the session should be a model that all agree represents the subject.

Using Data Modeling and CASE Tools

PC-based data modeling tools are starting to change the way models are built. CASE tools that deal with analysis (sometimes called upper CASE) usually have a data modeling component. Sometimes this component is a powerful data modeling tool, and other times it is little more than a means to push boxes around on a screen. Few are tied to a single data modeling technique or approach—so the data modeler is free to follow Chen, or NIAM, or any of a dozen other flavors of data modeling. However, very few tools are complete. Most offer a hodge-podge of various techniques and diagramming conventions. The result: while you can represent many approaches, few tools provide any discipline or alert the modeler to mistakes.

What are the advantages of using tools for data modeling? Tools allow you to

- Make changes to an existing diagram quickly.
- Cross reference objects, i.e., to print reports showing where attributes are used, etc.
- View objects:
  Neighborhood diagrams.
  Subject areas.
  Entity fragments.
- Project diagrams at meetings and facilitated joint sessions.
- Move the model to other phases or tools automatically.

When can the tool be of no advantage or an outright disadvantage? When

- Drawing the first version of a diagram—almost always, drawing the first version by hand is easier.
- It replaces thinking.
- Preparing documentation—dictionaries existed long before CASE tools.

Maintaining the Model

Clearly, tools and techniques are helpful in building a data model, but they are not as helpful in maintaining it. Imagine the following problem:

The banking application has moved from logical design through physical design and into coding. During coding it is discovered that while an account belongs to a customer, a customer can relate to another customer who does not have an account but about which the bank must save information. For example, the bank might have accounts for Thomas Rowley Real Estate Inc. and Thomas Rowley Travel Services Inc., but no account for the parent company, Thomas Rowley Holding Company. Unfortunately, available credit information is kept on the holding company, not the subsidiaries.

Because of the above, the designers changed the database design to allow

- Customers to be related to other customers.
- Customers who are not related to accounts.

If the documentation about the system is to be complete and accurate, someone must go back to the data model created during analysis (two phases ago) and update it to reflect these two changes.

Oddly enough, many organizations do not have a mechanism to accommodate maintaining a previously built data model. Frequently, data modelers are not informed about changes. Moreover, the data modeling team is likely to be disbanded once the original model has been completed. Nevertheless, if documentation is to be complete and accurate, and it must be if maintenance is to be hassle free, a mechanism is needed to ensure that the data model remains consistent with the application code.

Some emerging tools will eventually help alleviate this problem. Data modeling re-engineering tools, for example, can read a database schema and generate the data model from it. When these tools become more robust and available, they will ease much of the maintenance hassle.

The Two Logical Data Models

One of the dilemmas the data modeler faces relates to size and complexity. We know that a complete logical data model can have more than 200 entities and relationships and many hundreds of attributes. Add to that attributive and associative entities, subtypes/supertypes, and recursive relationships, and you have quite a complex diagram. Certainly too complex, technical, and confusing for some end users. End users need a simpler diagram, with fewer hieroglyphics, which represents data concepts that are more meaningful to them. On the other hand, system analysts and physical designers need detailed information about the data the organization or application uses. Their needs argue for a complete and exacting diagram.

The solution is actually quite easy. Create two models, both expressing the same data, but at two different levels of detail. The two models are

- The end-user logical data model, which

  Presents an end-user–oriented view.

  Reflects a high-level interpretation of the data.

  Includes only the basic entities and relationships with examples of attributes.

  Is usually "enterprise"-oriented.

- The detailed logical data model, which

  Represents a systems and business analyst view.

  Provides a low level of information.

  Gives detailed information about entities, relationships, and attributes.

  Is usually application-oriented.

A more technical and proper name for the end-user logical data model would probably be abstract data model. (Data abstraction is the deliberate suppression of irrelevant details to concentrate on relevant details.) However, the name end-user data model is used for two reasons. First, all data models are abstract, though the end-user data model will usually be more abstract than the detailed data model. Second, while the abstract data model might be a more apt name because it better defines what the model is, end-user data model better conveys the purpose and use of the model.

Timing and focus differentiate the two models. The end-user data model is created during the strategy, planning, and/or requirements definition phases, while the detailed data model is created during analysis or logical design (Fig. 5.8). Moreover, two very different audiences will be using the models, namely end-user staff and technical staff.

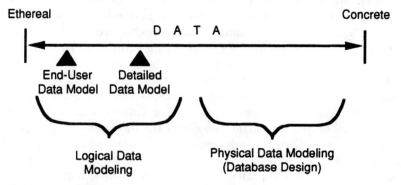

Figure 5.8 The data model continuum. The end-user and detailed logical data models represent different positions on the data model continuum.

As noted earlier, the end-user data model is usually developed during the planning stage or at the very beginning of analysis. Because it is at a very high level and more of a representation of interview notes than the product of careful analysis, it is often quite inaccurate. For example, it might include undetected derived data or processes that are incorrectly presented as data. It is hoped that these inaccuracies will be cleaned up during the analysis phase.

Any attributes uncovered while building the end-user model will probably be representative or examples. Modelers sometimes use the phrase "such as" to indicate that the entity will contain information such as account type or tax classification. Exact attribute identification will be left to the detailed data model.

Even though the end-user data model is a preliminary or first cut data model, it should not necessarily be discarded after development of the detailed data model. For many users, particularly end users, the end-user data model more closely represents the business with which they are familiar. It is often a good idea to keep the end-user data model up to date, but with fewer entities and relationships and simpler rules. Whereas the detailed data model would exclude derived data, have numerous subtypes, and express all relationships between entities, the end-user data model might only show major fundamental entities and significant relationships and might include derived entities such as Position and Customer Balance, if they prove to have significant meaning to users. The detailed data model is much closer to an "entity-relationship model" than the end-user model.

Remember: The emphasis is on communication (the first principle). The information needed to pass on to physical designers is very different from the information end users require. Whereas the detailed data model is necessary to build an application system, the end-user data model can be an important option if it contributes to end-user understanding of the project. Typically, the decision to produce only the detailed model or to produce both is left to the individual project team. Both models exist in popular methodologies. For example, for those familiar with Information Engineering, the end-user model relates closely to the enterprise model of the IE Planning phase; the detailed data model corresponds to the entity model of the Analysis phase.

Having two models is not as difficult as it first seems. The end-user data model is already a product of the planning phase; now you will simply be keeping it around and updated during analysis. Second, the two models are researched and built in exactly the same way. The techniques discussed in this and other chapters apply equally well to both models. In fact, in most cases, there will be no need to distinguish between the building of the two models except in the few cases where the handling of one is different from the other.

Data models during the interview process

A good way of communicating the important aspects of the data model is to tailor the model to the level of the audience. The end-user data model is simpler, technically less rigorous, and a superior diagram when working with end users. The detailed data model is a better diagram to use with technical staff.

The two models also provide an additional practical advantage. Some users refuse to review subtypes, attribute assignments, derived data exclusions, etc., no matter what technical arguments you put forward. The end-user data model allows these users to review a more personally relevant data model while still providing input for a "proper" detailed data model (Table 5.2).

Enterprise models

Some models are created not only to represent an application but also an entire organization. An enterprise model is one or more models used to document the processes and/or data for an entire organization, business, or enterprise. The enterprise process model is a high-level model that represents the major processes of the organization. The enterprise data model is a high-level logical data model of the information an organization uses and is very similar, if not identical, in structure to the end-user logical data model, though sometimes at a higher level of detail. With the exception of the level of detail, the processes to build an enterprise data model are identical to those described earlier in this chapter.

TABLE 5.2   Components of the End-User Data Model

Has	Usually Does Not Have
• Proper Entities	• Associatives • Attributive • Subtypes/supertypes
• Relationships • All Degrees	• Modality • Constraints
• Some Attributes	• Domains • Values
• Subject Areas	• Normalized Entities

What Not to Do and Why

People and change pose interesting—and difficult—obstacles when building the logical data model. A few pointers will ease the way.

Don't lose control of the project to users

Having the "right" relationship with the user staff is of utmost importance. In data modeling, the user must be heard. However, one of the most common causes of project failure is the loss of control of the assignment to the user, as in the example below.

A securities firm was redesigning its account processing system. During the data modeling exercises the issues of portfolios and positions came up. The business user wanted them on the data model, while the data modelers insisted that both were derived data and should not be part of the model. (Portfolios and positions are actually views of selected asset occurrences.) The user technical staff did not intervene and tactfully supported the business users, forcing the acceptance of the derived data on the data model.

Since portfolio and position were on the data model, none of the process modeling teams felt it was important to develop the processes to create the derived data. The unfortunate outcome was disharmony on the development team, uncertainty of who was in control, disruption and disagreement over what process modeling tasks had to be completed, and eventually the collapse of the project.

The moral of this story: Maintain control of the project and do that by

- Knowing what you are doing.
- Advertising what you are doing and why.
- Sticking to the plan.
- Making others stick to the plan by whatever means necessary.

Don't lose control of the project to technical staff

Losing control of data modeling to technical staff can be more disruptive and dangerous than losing control to a user. The problem is the "little knowledge" syndrome. Whereas end-user staff will usually admit that they have no idea what data modeling is, technical staff often feel they either know more about it than anybody or don't have to know about it because it is not important.

The remedy is up-front training on the advantages of data modeling and, perhaps what is more important, the dangers of not data modeling correctly.

Don't become dependent on tools or techniques

Too many organizations welcome new methodologies, techniques, and tools without fully understanding what the consequences will be. For example:

The development team at Rossetti & Siddall Publishing decided that a CASE tool was necessary. After getting the tool, the team charged into a major application and in no time was up a creek. The team quickly discovered that having a tool does not mean the underlying techniques are understood, nor does the tool make up for lack of expertise in knowing how to use the techniques.

Late, but not totally discouraged, the team decided to learn about data modeling and other necessary techniques, but success still eluded them. At last they learned that knowing techniques does not mean they have an approach or methodology for developing systems.

The moral of the story: Understand the technique before picking a methodology or tool (Fig. 5.9).

Techniques follow an approach. For example, this book focuses on the entity-relationship approach to data modeling. However, tools can usually support a number of approaches, and techniques can be bundled (though not all are) into methodologies.

The right approach to mastering the lot is to focus on techniques first, then methodologies, and last tools. To alter the sequence can invite excessive learning-curve pain and poor system workmanship (Fig. 5.10).

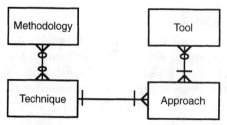

Figure 5.9 The relationships between system development components.

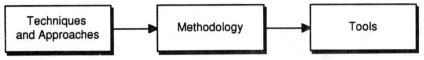

Figure 5.10 Introduce techniques first, tools last.

Don't be concerned about which comes first— the data model or the process model

No one disagrees with the notion that it's important to decide which comes first. The determination, however, is usually not in the hands of the data modelers.

While this might sound like heresy to some, data modeling works equally well whether the methodology is data driven or process driven—if applied properly. The issue is not whether systems can be built with one approach and not the other. In fact, the difference between the two methodology approaches only relates to the ease or difficulty of designing the system.

In practice, the distinction between the two quickly becomes moot, since neither one can be accomplished independently of the other. Data cannot be uncovered without looking at processes, and processes cannot be identified without looking at data. It's sort of like walking with your legs tied together with a 1 ft rope. It is possible to lead with your left foot or your right, but before long you must bring up the other foot before the first can go any further.

Don't become bogged down in endless analysis

Modeling is difficult. The logical data modeler must juggle hundreds of data objects. Moreover, data modeling is only a small part of the systems development process. Each object is examined repeatedly as new data is uncovered. Thus, developing and keeping the data model correct is truly a daunting but necessary task. However, because incomplete or inaccurate logical data models can be linked to disastrous application development efforts, the prudent systems analyst would be wise to ensure that the data model is as correct as possible. While an inaccurate object in a process model might cause the incorrect execution of a business function, an incorrect data object can cause the misexecution of many processes.

Some project staff, however, go to the other extreme and get bogged down in endless analysis. In the quest for perfection, some analysts never finish the model(s) at all. In such cases, the project is frequently put on the back burner or canceled, and the cause for the shutdown is listed as anything from end-user relation problems to functional complexity.

Data modelers get bogged down for a number of reasons. They

- Don't recognize that the benefits to be achieved by additional modeling are diminishing
- Fear moving ahead because they
  Have analysis paralysis—perfectionism
  Are afraid to start the next step
- Lack confidence in the model
- Have a poor understanding of how the model will be used

Complete analysis is essential, but knowing when enough is enough requires judgment. Analysis should be called to a halt when

- New information provides little additional value.
- Users and analysts are quibbling over unimportant items.
- There is sufficient information to move on to the next phase.

Then put a "stake" in the ground and freeze the data model:

- No new changes.
- Model goes into maintenance mode.
- A data model change control process is established.

Evaluate all changes to see if/when they should be applied to the model/project. Changes should be divided into three categories:

- Immediate change to the data model and all work products
- Attention needed at the end of the current phase
- Attention required at some future release of the application (Fig. 5.11)

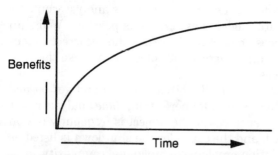

Figure 5.11 Benefits gains can diminish over time.

The People—and the Rules

Putting together a constructive team to collect and properly analyze an organization's data is a difficult task. Surprisingly or not, many system professionals do not cherish the thought of data modeling for a number of reasons. Understanding why will help you manage the project more effectively.

First, as previously noted, data modeling is a highly abstract process and not all systems professionals have the required ability to perform it. Clearly, if individuals cannot conceptualize, all the techniques and tools in the world will not help them data model. Also, data modeling is nondeterministic. There is no right answer, since there are a number of different ways a business can be modeled. However, there certainly are wrong answers. Some system professionals have trouble with the subjective nature of the technique in a profession they see as stressing objectivity.

Second, data modeling represents change, and change is often the biggest threat to people. Ironically, systems professionals have been pushing change on others for years. They have preached automation as the solution to the cost and time constraints with which many organizations struggle. Yet, systems is still one of the most manually intensive areas in many companies today.

When it is data processing's turn to face change, just as many heels dig in as did two decades ago when payrolls were being automated. The issue: Change in the form of new techniques and tools threatens the livelihood of the staff—sometimes overnight. That is why many organizations have a special "data team" to handle the data modeling tasks, and why data modeling is often the first item to be sacrificed when schedules push against progress.

Third, logical data modeling requires judgment, but the criteria for that judgment are often left to chance. By default, the data modeler is left to follow the "rational man" principle—do what a rational person would do in the same situation. Unfortunately, even if you can find a rational person, the odds are against his or her knowing how to data model. A better principle is to do what a logical data modeling expert would do in the same situation. This, of course, assumes you know what a logical data modeling expert would do.

The best approach is to apply the three logical data modeling principles to the situation. Ask the question, "What should I do to improve the communication, logical representation, and/or sufficient granularity of the model?" If adding or removing some feature improves the utility of the model as defined by the principles, then do it. If not, then do not do it.

Finally, a set of rules or guidelines is critical to the success of any data modeling project, and the ground rules should be established *before* the process starts to avoid useless battles. Arguments become less intense and less detrimental to progress when they are related to abstract rules. For example, the statement, "Do not model derived data," is abstract—without emotional ties to a real life situation. On the other hand, "*Portfolio* is derived data and will, therefore, not be modeled," is grounded in reality, and arguments about whether or not to observe this rule can evoke an emotional response.

The successful data modeler will be prepared for these possibilities.

Logical Data Modeling Guidelines

*"Rules are for the obedience of fools and the
guidance of wise men."*   DAVID OGILVY

"He jests at scars that never felt a wound."
     SHAKESPEARE

The heart of this (and the next) chapter and the soul of this book are
based on a singular premise: Since no exacting formulas exist to guide
the data modeler every step of the way, a body of knowledge in the form
of best practices (guidelines and rules of thumb) is necessary to support the successful completion of the logical data model—and to reduce
or eliminate roadblocks and problems.

The guidelines that follow should be viewed as a foundation upon
which to develop more specific data modeling rules for a given project.
Some of the guidelines only apply to the end-user model, and others to
the detailed logical data model (Table 6.1). Those that apply to both do
not always do so equally. Examine each in detail and make the changes
you feel are necessary for your given situation. You may even wish to
add or delete guidelines. When you are finished, present them to the
project team as a team or organization document. Encourage feedback
before the project starts.

When there is consensus, the guidelines should become the
"standard" used by the team. Any subsequent changes to the standard should go through some change control process which ensures
that the decision to make a change is based on principle and not
on accommodating a pet data interpretation of one of the team
members. For example, if a guideline states that the derived data
attribute PORTFOLIO should not be on the model, the change con-

TABLE 6.1   Applying Guidelines to Data Models

Data Modeling Reference	End-User Model	Detailed Model
Abbreviations	√	√
Clarity	√	√
Compound Identifiers		√
Conceptual Integrity		√
Conjunctive Relationships		√
Data Value Differentiated Entities/Attributes		√
Data Values	√	√
Derived Data		√
Discrete Attributes	√	√
Embedded Attributes	√	√
Empty Entities		√
Exclusive Relationships	√	√
Extraneous Relationships	√	√
Foreign Keys	√	√
Group Data Items		√
Identifiers		√
Level of Abstraction		√
Many-to-Many Relationships	√	√
Naming Objects	√	√
N-ary Relationships	√	√
Normalization		√
Null Attributes	√	√
Optional Relationships	√	√
Presentation Data	√	√
Primary Keys	√	√
Process Data	√	√
Repeating Groups		√
Subject Areas	√	√
Substitution Data		√
Supertypes and Subtypes	√	√
Transient Data		√

Note: √ Indicates to which model a guideline applies. Not all guidelines apply to both data models.

trol team should make sure that a subsequent change to allow its representation is based on sound reasoning and not just on making the advocate of PORTFOLIO happy.

For ease of use and reference, this chapter is organized like a glossary or encyclopedia, i.e., the entries are in alphabetical order. The guildelines consist of a one or two sentence description followed by a discussion and, in some cases, examples that illustrate the use of the guideline. At the end of the chapter, you will find a list that aligns the guidelines with the principles offered in Chapter 2.

Abbreviations

Abbreviations should be kept to a minimum, and when used, they should be meaningful to the end user. Standard computer-based abbreviations should not be confused with abbreviations used in modeling data. Standard abbreviations are created for use in operating systems, computer languages, file managers, and DBMSs, which limit the length of field, record, file, and program names. They permit text to physically fit into computer-managed directories.

Name length restrictions, however, are physical design issues and not part of logical analysis. What's important to logical analysis is meaning. As such, the distinction between computer-based abbreviations and legitimate end-user abbreviations created for logical data modeling is significant. For example, in the securities processing business, "DK," which stands for "*Don't Know*," is the recognized symbol for an unknown or unidentifiable transaction and, therefore, an acceptable end-user abbreviation. However, if you've identified CUSTOMER FINAL PRE-PAYMENT DATE as an attribute, it should be written as CUSTOMER FINAL PRE-PAYMENT DATE (meaningful to the end user) and not CUS_FIN_PREPMT_DTE (required to satisfy a name length restriction).

The developer, however, should be sensitive to the unfortunate fact that system development tools usually have name length limits that sometimes can force the use of nonbusiness abbreviations. If you must use abbreviations, keep them in English. Avoid schemes such as stripping out vowels to shorten words, which usually result in unrecognizable and unpronounceable abbreviations. For example, a vowel-dropping scheme would turn VENDOR ASSIGNED USER CODE into the horribly mashed VNDR ASGND USR CD. Stick with simple English abbreviations and standard initials such as

Word(s)	Abbreviation/initials
Customer	Cust
Account	Acct
Lysergic acid diethylamide	LSD
Pennsylvania	PA, Penna

A good set of approved abbreviations for the logical data model will make the transition from the logical to physical design easier. Publishing a list of acceptable abbreviations is particularly useful. However, recognize that the list will not be exhaustive and will have to be constantly updated. Ideally, the process of adding entries should be simple and quick. Avoiding long review processes and acceptance committees is highly recommended.

Clarity

Remove confusing objects from the data model. This is a "judgment call" rule. But if you remember that the dual purpose of a data model is to

- Feed back information to end users, who verify the model
- Communicate end-user information to physical designers

then you can better judge whether objects added to the model, or left out, contribute to communication or subtract from it. Examples of extraneous objects are unnecessary sub-supertypes, extraneous relationships, and unnecessary entities.

Let's look at the example in Fig. 6.1. The Flotsam and Jetsam Imported Goods Company data model contains extraneous data objects:

- Since the participating entities and connectivity for the relationships Buy and Return are identical, they should be represented by the single relationship Buy and Return.
- Since the subtypes Retail and Wholesale have identical attributes and relationships, they are superfluous and should be eliminated.

Clarity is the reason the majority of the entries, such as derived data, embedded attributes, and multiple relationships, are in this book.

Compound Identifiers

Compound identifiers are acceptable, and the position of the attributes within the identifier is unimportant. Compound identifiers present a unique situation. Assume attributes 'A' and 'B' form a compound identifier. The order in which they are presented is unimportant for logical

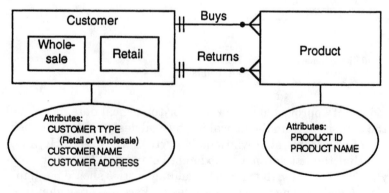

Figure 6.1 Model containing extraneous objects: Flotsam and Jetsam Imported Goods.

data modeling purposes. Thus, the identifier can be represented as 'A*B' (attribute 'A' and attribute 'B') or 'B*A' (attribute 'B' and attribute 'A').

However, the order can be critical for database designers, since the sequence of fields in compound keys can be the major determinant in index and data storage clustering. Because of this importance to database design, some logical data modelers feel compelled to identify the sequence. This is a mistake for two reasons:

- The physical determination of whether a compound key should be 'A*B' or 'B*A' is decided by examining how the data is used (process analysis) not by its definition (data analysis). Since logical data modeling is concerned with data and not processes, the data modeler is the wrong person to make this determination.

- Issues of index and data storage clustering are physical design issues and not relevant to logical data modeling.

How keys should be organized or data clustered is an issue that should be left to database designers in the physical design phase. (See Identifiers entry in this chapter.)

Conceptual Integrity

Maintain the integrity of logical data modeling concepts, even if the tool you are using makes it difficult. Tools can often confuse or corrupt logical data modeling concepts. While it will be necessary to observe the data modeling conventions followed or required by the development tool you are using, do not lose sight of the correct logical data modeling concepts and why they are important.

An example can best illustrate this point. Is the relationship entity pair 'Customers Buy Cars,' one relationship or two? The answer, of course, is one. To confirm this, just examine how people speak. You will hear that a husband and wife have *a* relationship, not that the husband has one relationship and the wife another. People also speak about *the* relationship between the United States and Japan.

Unfortunately, that is not the way some CASE tools work. Many tools would treat the automobile example as two separate relationships ('Customers Buy Cars' and 'Cars Are Bought by Customers') and require that two dictionary entries be completed, e.g., two names, two definitions (Fig. 6.2).

This problem is more persistent in tools that consider all relationships binary or in tools using a line as the graphic convention for a relationship. The problem is less likely to occur in tools that permit n-ary relationships or the use of a diamond as a relationship symbol (Fig. 6.3).

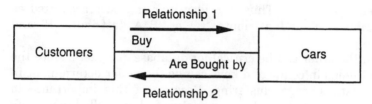

Figure 6.2   A binary relationship treated as two separate relationships.

As an example, let's take the n-ary relationship, 'Customers Buy Cars from Dealers.' Is this one relationship, two, three, or six? The correct answer is, of course, one, but various tools will require anywhere from one to six relationships as the definition (Fig. 6.4).

You might have to bend your principles in order to use available tools. If you have to compromise the implementation of the logical data model, remember to keep the conceptual integrity of your model strong, and document all tool-induced compromises in the data dictionary.

Conjunctive Relationships

Allow conjunctive "and" relationships, since they are a legitimate end-user concept. Conjunctive relationships stipulate that if entity type 'A' is related to entity type 'B,' then 'A' must also be related to entity type 'C.' But few data models include conjunction in their model for any one of three reasons:

- Conjunctive relationships are not common in businesses.
- Few DBMSs directly allow their implementation.
- Most modelers don't know that the concept of conjunction exists.

The first reason might be true. The third reason is all too true. The second reason, however, is the misplaced physical design issue again.

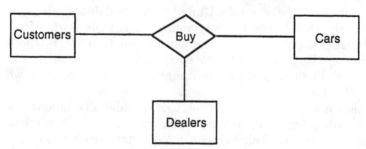

Figure 6.3   The single n-ary relationship "buy" links three separate entities.

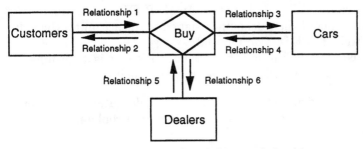

Figure 6.4   N-ary relationship treated as six binary relationships.

True as it might be that most DBMSs do not allow easy implementation of conjunction, the argument is, nonetheless, misplaced in logical design. If conjunction is a real end-user concept, model it. If it is important to the business, it can always be implemented through application code if the DBMS does not support it.

Data Value–Differentiated Entities and Attributes

Do not allow data values to differentiate or define entities or other attributes. This guideline is the reciprocal of modeling data values. Data value differentiated–entities and attributes occur when the value of an attribute is used to define an entity type or another attribute type. For example, imagine the following:

The order entry data model for a consumer products firm includes the entity Product with the attributes PRODUCT SOURCE and MANUFACTURER. If the value of PRODUCT SOURCE is "Internal," then the attribute MANUFACTURER contains the plant location which created the product. However, if the value of PRODUCT SOURCE is "Purchased," then the attribute MANUFACTURER contains the name of the manufacturer which made the item.

Product Name	Product Source	Manufacturer
Can Opener	Internal	High Street Plant
Vegamatic	Purchased	Ronco Manufacturing

In this example the definition of MANUFACTURER is dependent on the value of PRODUCT SOURCE.

Another example of a data value–differentiated entity would be when the entity Customer contains the name and address of a customer if the value of the attribute CUSTOMER TYPE is "Commercial," or information about the salesman assigned to the account if the value of CUSTOMER TYPE is "Confidential."

In both cases the definition of an attribute or entity is determined by the value of an attribute. This is an error because it

- Eliminates or hides from the data model the definitions of real business entities, attributes, and relationships and replaces them with attribute values.

- Makes an entity or attribute a property or characteristic of a data value when, by definition, data values are characteristics or properties of attributes, and attributes are characteristics or properties of entities.

There is one case where this rule appears to be broken but in fact it is not. A subtype will often have a type or role attribute which defines the subtype and thus determines the properties of the subtype (see Duplicate Subtype/Supertype "Type" Data in Chapter 7). But closer examination will reveal that the "Type" attribute in a subtype is actually a role determinant and should, for the purposes of this guideline, be considered an attribute of the supertype.

Some readers will note that this is very similar to the restrictions imposed by normalization's second normal form. (Also see Data Values and Level of Abstraction in this chapter.)

Data Values

Do not model the values of data. Data models model data objects, not the values of data objects. Even experienced modelers have trouble with this simple concept. Understandably, values can show up in the end-user model, where they are presented by users as separate data. However, after some analysis, values should be eliminated. Take this case, for example.

During the creation of the end-user model, the users make a distinction between commercial and government clients. If the client is the government, a 30 days net payment rule does not apply. However, if a commercial account is not paid within 30 days, a second notice is sent.

The modelers decide to create two entities—Commercial Client and Government Client.

The error that was made was letting the data value of an attribute CLIENT TYPE differentiate entity types. In the above example, the modelers have uncovered nothing to distinguish the entities Commercial and Government. Rather, all they have discovered is that the model will need the attribute CLIENT TYPE to contain the value "Commercial" or "Government" so that a process can distinguish the two. In the future, if attributes are uncovered which relate only to a commercial or government client, then a supertype/subtype structure or even two separate entities might be necessary.

A quick test to determine if values are being modeled is to examine the entity and attribute names. If the entity or attribute name is a proper noun, it is a good bet that what has been modeled is the value of an attribute. To avoid this problem you may need to replace one attribute with two or more (Table 6.2).

A Yes/No-type attribute (e.g., U.S. CITIZEN, which limits the acceptable data values to "Yes" or "No") is an excellent candidate for causing confusion. Using citizenship as the example, a better approach would be to model a CITIZENSHIP attribute for which the acceptable values are the names of countries.

Derived Data

Avoid placing derived data on the data model, though it should be in the data dictionary. Derived data items are data objects that can be calculated from primitive data in the model or from other derived data. For example, if an accounts payable system stores data on each purchase, then the data item TOTAL AMOUNT ORDERED is considered derived, since it is arrived at by adding each of the individual orders. TOTAL AMOUNT ORDERED is the sum of the values in all the occurrences of the INVOICE AMOUNT data element.

There are three traditional arguments against modeling derived data. It:

- Is redundant
- Takes up database storage space
- Limits the choices of physical designers

TABLE 6.2   Examples of Invalid and Valid Attribute Types

Invalid Attribute Types	Valid Attribute Types
IBM MODEL	VENDOR, COMPUTER MODEL
U.S. TAX	COUNTRY, COUNTRY TAX
S&P RATING	RATING SERVICE, RATING
ZIP CODE	POSTAL CODE

Note: Do not confuse attribute values and attribute types.

Many modelers would say that TOTAL AMOUNT ORDERED is redundant since it can be calculated from the individual orders. This redundancy is undesirable since it can lead to inconsistencies if the value in TOTAL AMOUNT ORDERED does not equal the sum of the INVOICE AMOUNTs. Put simply, the argument is that if data is stored only once, you will not have inconsistencies.

The second argument is that because it is redundant, derived data unnecessarily takes up storage space (i.e., on disk or tape) and increases storage costs.

The third argument goes as follows: The decision about whether a data object should be stored or calculated is a physical design issue. The relevant questions deal with the cost/benefit tradeoffs between the storage space needed to house the redundant data and the I/O and CPU cycles necessary to calculate it every time it is needed. If the derived data is left out of the data model, the physical designer, it is argued, can always turn it into stored data if he/she deems it desirable. However, if derived data is part of the data model, the physical designer might not know it is derived and will, therefore, not know that the option to store or calculate the data exists. Thus, placing derived data on the data model limits the options open to the designer.

These arguments are not very compelling. The redundancy argument ignores the fact that redundant data can only be inconsistent when some or all of it is wrong. But if it is wrong, it is wrong whether it is in the model once or multiple times. Redundancy, in fact, points out incorrect data that might otherwise go undetected.

It is true that storing derived data in the database will increase storage costs. However, the argument is misplaced. Issues such as database storage should not be part of logical design and should be left to physical design.

The third argument would be correct if there was no other way to communicate the derived nature of the data object to the physical designers. However, there are numerous alternative methods of saying that data is derived without dropping it from the data model.

The notion that those who argue against derived data also believe it should not exist is a common misconception. Derived data opponents are merely against placing it on the data model. They would say that it is really the restatement of data that already exists on the model. To include it in the model would be to corrupt the fundamental or atomic nature of the model.

A more compelling reason not to model derived data is simply that derived data is not data at all; rather, it represents a process.

Derived data as process

Derived data does not really behave like data. For example, you can completely understand primitive data with a definition, but to understand derived data you need a formula or algorithm. Let's look at the example:

TOTAL AMOUNT ORDERED for ACCOUNT NUMBER = '1234' is the sum of the values of INVOICE AMOUNT for that account.

To understand TOTAL AMOUNT ORDERED, you need to see a formula or action diagram. However, formulas and action diagrams are properties of processes, not data. So the real problem with putting derived data on a data model is that it is not data at all. It is, instead, a process for applying a set of rules to data values to calculate other data values (Fig. 6.5).

Note in the example that the value of TOTAL AMOUNT ORDERED is dependent on applying a process to the individual values of INVOICE AMOUNT. If one of the latter changes, then TOTAL AMOUNT ORDERED must change.

Primitive data can be understood by looking at its definition

    Attribute Definition

        Attribute Name: ACCOUNT NUMBER

        Definition: An identifier of an approved account of any status. The Accounts Payable Dept. assigns account numbers.

However, derived data needs a formula or algorithm

    Action Diagram

        Calculate Total Amount Ordered

            Get Accounts Payable Entity

                For each ACCOUNT NUMBER

                Sum INVOICE AMOUNT giving TOTAL AMOUNT ORDERED

                End

            End

        End

Figure 6.5 Derived data as a process.

Recognizing that derived data looks more like a process than data is important to systems development. Just giving a definition when a formula is required will not do. An action diagram or some similar process modeling construct is needed to properly communicate the nature of the derived data object to the physical designers.

Derived data and physical database design

From a physical database design perspective, whether derived data is stored in the database or calculated every time it is needed is a mathematical question. The physical database designer will calculate the resource costs to store the derived data, compare them with the resource costs to calculate it every time it is needed, and choose the less expensive option. The only real question is how does the physical database designer know the data is derived?

If derived data is not on the data model, then how is it represented in the physical database design process? This can be a problem. Many data modelers make the mistake of so efficiently excluding derived data from development documentation that physical designers do not even know it exists.

The solution to this problem is relatively simple: derived data should exist as a process with data flows and data stores and be represented in the data dictionary. The dictionary should explicitly state that the attribute is derived and give the name of the process (action diagram) that defines it. If your only data dictionary is tied to a data modeling tool, and since some data modeling tools require that all attributes be associated with an entity, the data modeler might have to create one or more dummy entities to house derived data (Fig. 6.6).

If derived data is properly documented, then the physical database designers will know that derived data exists, where it is used, and how it is defined. They will then be in a position to intelligently introduce it into the physical database design process.

Discrete Attributes

An attribute should exist in the model once and only once. Placing an attribute in the model more than once is usually a sign of confusion about the name and/or definition of the attribute or a misunderstanding about logical data modeling. Nevertheless, having stated the rule, modelers must be mindful of some exceptions:

- If the data modeling tool being used requires the modeling of a foreign key, then an attribute might appear more than once, since it may appear as a foreign key. Following its first occurrence, however, an attribute should *only* reappear as a foreign key. (See entry for Foreign Keys in this chapter.)

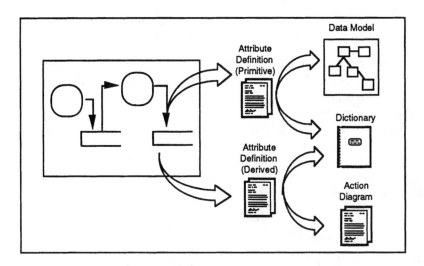

Figure 6.6 Location of derived data.

- Certain attributes might *seem* to appear more than once, but this is usually because the attribute name is less specific than it should be. For example, generic names such as DATE, AMOUNT, or TOTAL AMOUNT, which may appear in several places, are OK as long as everyone understands that DATE in the Customer Billing entity is a different attribute from the DATE in the Product Price Schedule entity. In this example, everyone has agreed to call the attribute not by its name but by its domain. This, however, can cause confusion down the road when some user tries to execute a relational DBMS "join" on unrelated attributes. To be more accurate, the attributes should be named CUSTOMER BILLING DATE and PRODUCT PRICE SCHEDULE DATE.

- A variation of the above can occur with codes and indicators. For example, a number of entities might have the attribute, STATUS CODE. This is acceptable, though perhaps not in the best form, if the domains (all the acceptable values, such as "Active," "Inactive," and "Closed") are all identical. If the domains are different, then the attributes must have different names.

- A differentiator attribute is often needed in each subtype of a sub-supertype construct to differentiate the role the entity is playing (see Supertypes and Subtypes entry in this chapter and Duplicate Supertype "Type" Data in Chap. 7).

- Identifier attributes sometimes appear in more than one entity. For example, EMPLOYEE NUMBER might be an identifier or part of the identifier in the entities Employee, Employee Address and

Employee History. However, a better solution is to define the entity as attributive and remove the redundant data.

Be careful. An attribute appearing more than once could signal a number of other problems such as modeling data values, improper use of supertypes and subtypes, or an attempt to get around the restriction on repeating groups.

Concatenating the entity name to the attribute name (such as using "dot" notation in Entity Name.Attribute Name as in CUSTOMER. ADDRESS) is not an acceptable method of making an attribute name unique. Attribute names must stand on their own, independent of the entity with which they are associated.

Embedded Attributes

Do not allow embedded attributes. Embedded attributes are data items with other attributes "buried" in them. This is usually done to make the compound attribute unique or to combine two or more attributes into a group data item. For example, the data item ACCOUNT NUMBER for a bank might be made up of a branch code and a sequence number within a branch. The branch code is needed because the sequence numbers may be repeated from branch to branch. The combination of branch code and sequence number uniquely identify an account within the organization.

The above discussion actually consists of two separate issues. The first deals with what has to be done to make an identifier unique. Making identifiers unique is an important physical design issue. Without uniqueness, there is no guarantee that the right record is updated. However, whereas identifying unique attributes is an important logical data modeling function, making entity occurrences unique is not.

The second issue is concerned with ensuring that all attributes are treated as attributes. The danger that logical data modelers face when they get involved with this physical issue is that valuable logical design data could be lost. This can occur when a value is embedded in another attribute, in which case one might assume that there is no necessity to "duplicate" it elsewhere. Thus, referring back to the branch code example, even if you are convinced that branch code will be embedded in ACCOUNT NUMBER, the attribute BRANCH CODE should still be modeled separately. If it is not, and the physical designers choose a different method to make an account unique, branch information could be lost.

This problem can become sticky when the user insists that the attribute BRANCH CODE is not needed because the value, branch code, is the first two digits of ACCOUNT NUMBER. The data modeler must ensure that in spite of these problems, all relevant data, such as BRANCH CODE, are modeled.

Empty Entities

When the data model is finished, no entities should exist without attributes, nor should they have only one attribute in them (especially if the one attribute is a code or an indicator) or only identifiers. Empty entities indicate that either the model is not complete or that some of the entities are wrong. This problem is more common than one might assume. It is usually a consequence of the following:

Early in the process the modelers meet with users and develop a list of entities and some attributes. This initial work becomes the end-user model.

After additional work the detailed model is almost complete, but three entities are empty (have no attributes). The decision is made to keep the entities on the model for the following reasons:

- The entities are important to the users, who are likely to ask for them if they are missing.

- The modelers sense they may have missed the attributes that make up these entities and fear that as soon as the entities are removed, some-one will uncover the missing attributes.

Whereas empty attributes are acceptable in the end-user model, best practices dictate that the detailed model represent verified data and that open issues be excluded or identified as unresolved. (Also see Single Attribute Entities in Chap. 7.)

Exclusive Relationships

Allow "exclusive or" relationships, since they are a legitimate end-user concept. Some modelers disallow exclusive relationships (Fig. 6.7) because

- Most tools and DBMSs simply do not support *exclusive or*.

- Exclusion can sometimes allow null values in primary keys.

It is certainly true that very few data modeling tools support *exclusive or* relationships and no major DBMS does. Nevertheless,

- Physical design issues should be kept out of logical design and stay in physical design where they belong.

- Data modeling should not limit itself to what is supported by a physical DBMS or tool. For example, if the need for exclusion is sufficient,

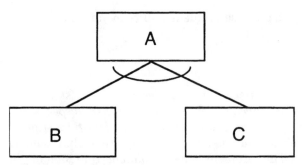

Figure 6.7 Exclusive relationship. An occurrence of 'A' can be related to either one 'B' or one 'C,' but not both.

the physical designers could decide to implement it through application code. This would not be possible if the need were not conveyed to them in logical data modeling.

This last argument raises an important point. If a particular DBMS or file management system does not support a certain feature, the developers still have the option to include the features with application code. But they can only do this if they know that the feature is desired, and that is communicated to them through the logical data and process models.

As for nulls, contrary to what some relational database advocates believe, exclusive relationships do not require nulls in primary keys, but they are possible if the primary key is also the foreign key (see entries on Null Attributes, Primary Keys, and Foreign Keys). However, do not concern yourself with this argument, because it is misplaced. Issues such as null values and keys (primary or foreign) are physical design issues and not relevant to a discussion of logical data modeling.

Extraneous Relationships

Avoid extraneous relationships. Extraneous relationships are primarily a diagramming issue. If redundant or extraneous relationships are included on the diagram, the diagram can become confusing and messy. Leaving them out, particularly in the end-user model, can make the diagram more readable (Fig. 6.8).

Foreign Keys

Although perhaps unavoidable with some tools, defining relationships through foreign keys should be discouraged. A foreign key is not a legit-

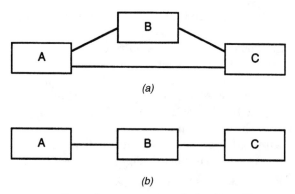

Figure 6.8 Removing extraneous relationships. The transitive relationship between 'A' and 'C' could be removed.

imate logical data modeling concept. It is a physical design issue, tied to the relational model and supported by only a few relational database management systems.

The term "foreign key" comes from relational theory. Unfortunately, some modelers and tools use foreign keys as a way of defining relationships between entities.

Relational fans hold your ears. OK? Well, for the rest of you, a foreign key is a type of pointer (actually a symbolic key) to another tuple (relational record). By using pointers, relational systems perform "joins" and—dare I say it—navigate. This is how it works.

If an Account occurrence is related to one or more Invoice occurrences in a one-to-many relationship, then a "linking" data element must exist in both records. The value of the data element ACCOUNT NUMBER in Invoice must be the same as the value of ACCOUNT NUMBER in the Account relation. Thus, when you want account information and invoices for account 1234, the system can go to the appropriate occurrences of Account and Invoice using the specified value "1234" for attribute ACCOUNT NUMBER (Fig. 6.9). (The linking data elements need not have the same name.)

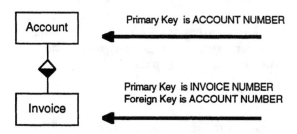

Figure 6.9 Foreign keys.

Simple. It just requires a bit of redundant data to "point" to related records.

While this is all well and good, it simply has no relevance to logical data modeling—except in one awkward situation. Some data modeling tools are designed to primarily, or exclusively, work with relational systems. The only way to relate entity 'A' with entity 'B' with these products is to specify a foreign key. If you are using one of these tools, you will have to make the best of the situation.

Interestingly enough, after all the relational talk, many relational DBMSs do not, at this time anyway, support foreign keys. (See Identifiers entry.)

Group Data Items

Group data items are to be avoided, since they can hide information about attributes and entity relationships. Attributes should always be atomic (nondecomposable) data objects, i.e., objects at the lowest level of data abstraction used by an organization. This is to contrast them with group data items or data aggregates. For example, CUSTOMER ADDRESS is a group data item if you also need to know about CUSTOMER STATE.

Most modelers use the term aggregate to refer to a group data item and element to refer to an atomic data item. For example, CUSTOMER ADDRESS would be the aggregate and CUSTOMER STREET, CUSTOMER STATE, and CUSTOMER POSTAL CODE would be the elements. Aggregates provide a shorthand term for a list of attributes. Attributes are always elements and never aggregates. This is because developers need to know all the details about the data, and aggregates hide detail information by burying multiple attributes in one named object.

Sometimes it is not clear whether a data object is an attribute or an aggregate. For example, is DATE an attribute or an aggregate for MONTH, DAY, and YEAR? In this case, the convention is to treat DATE as the attribute even though an application might need to reference part of a date, such as year.

Certain database management systems, such as relational systems, do not allow group or aggregate data items, so it is best to eliminate them during logical data modeling rather than have them eliminated later by some physical designer, who might get it wrong. The best advice is to avoid group data items whenever possible.

Identifiers

The designation of one or more attributes as an entity identifier is encouraged and should be specified if the identifier is a legitimate end-user concept. However, "assigning" an identifier or arbitrarily making

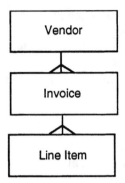

Figure 6.10 Accounts payable data model.

one identifier "primary" for systems purposes is wrong and should be discouraged. An identifier is an attribute or group of attributes that uniquely determines an entity. Some system development techniques and tools require that all entities have identifiers, and some go further and require that one identifier be designated "prime." The terms they tend to use are "keys" and "primary keys." Keys and primary keys are an important part of physical database design and are required by some database management systems. However, these physical issues are inappropriate here.

If there is more than one identifier in an entity, some authors recommend arbitrarily identifying one as the prime identifier and the others as secondary identifiers. But it is absurd and by definition an arbitrary decision to pick one identifier over another as the prime identifier. Modelers should not build arbitrariness into a model.

More importantly, identifiers are not needed for all entities. Take the example of an accounts payable system (Fig. 6.10).

What is the identifier of Line Item (Table 6.3)?

To create a unique Line Item identifier, some analysts designate a system generated key such as a sequential number (a physical design issue) or use an identifier from another entity. For example, Invoice Number could be the identifier of Invoice and, concatenated with Line

TABLE 6.3 Finding the Identifier

Identifier	Description
• LINE NUMBER ?	• No, it is not unique
• INVOICE NUMBER and LINE NUMBER?	• It is unique, but requires the duplication of INVOICE NUMBER in two entities
• PRODUCT ORDERED, LINE NUMBER, and DATE?	• Not necessarily unique

Number, the identifier of Line Item. Neither the system generated key nor the borrowed identifier are good ideas, since they are artificial and fictitious. If there is no legitimate identifier for an entity, leave it "identifier-less."

The following two examples illustrate instances where nonidentified data might exist.

Example 1

Good Health Insurance Co. wishes to create new weight-height tables for its actuarial department. To do this, they will send to each resident of several randomly selected towns an information package and a postcard to fill out and return. Anonymity is guaranteed. The postcard information contains fields for

Height	Sex
Weight	Race
Date of Birth	

The cards will be entered in Good Health's database with no end-user identifier.

Example 2

Fair Play Inc. provides a service that looks at other companies' personnel records and reports if they show any indication of racial, gender, or age discrimination. The program works as follows:

Clients send to Fair Play their personnel records of all employees minus any identifying information. For example, data would include:

Race	Years with firm
Sex	Education
Date of Birth	Position in firm
Weight	Years in position
Height	Salary

Information not included:

Name	Employee Number
Social Security No.	Address
Phone Number	

Fair Play's database to store this information will have no end-user identifier.

Identifiers that are a legitimate part of the business, however, should be modeled. Some system development tools insist that a non-business identifier be assigned, which requires data and/or processes that are not part of the business. To alter the business or the representation of the business to satisfy a development tool is misleading, unnecessary, and simply wrong.

Level of Abstraction

Make the data model as abstract as possible while still fully and adequately describing the subject. The Data Values entry in this chapter illustrated how some modelers model the values of data rather than the data types. This could result in having the data model represent only a subset of the total possible occurrences of the data type, leaving a prematurely aging data model requiring possible frequent changes and updates.

Models can be more accurate and stay up to date longer when their structure is abstract. For example, using the more abstract attribute POSTAL CODE (and its more abstract domain) rather than the less abstract attribute ZIP CODE can extend the life of the model beyond the first time an international address is stored. Likewise, the more abstract entity Employee can accommodate more and varied attributes and relationships than the more concrete entity Hourly Worker. Abstraction allows a data model to express more diverse data and do so with fewer data objects.

However, taken too far, abstraction could be just as damaging, if not more so, than being too concrete. Abstracting the entities Employees, Customers, and Regulators to the single entity People is probably excessive since it hides the basic and different relationships of the three groups within the organization. Likewise, combining the high school grade system attributes GRADE, EFFORT, and ABILITY into COMMENTS causes loss of meaning and potential utility.

The challenge is to forgo premature aging of a data model by making sure the data objects are sufficiently abstract, while ensuring that anyone reading the data model will know what the subject is about. When the name and/or description of the object starts to become meaningless, then abstraction has gone too far.

Taken to its extreme, excessive abstraction could collapse an entire data model into what some call a TUAKASUDM (commonly pronounced "too-ack-a-sue-dum") or The Universal All Knowing All Seeing Ultimate Data Model (Fig. 6.11). A TUAKASUDM can represent any complex and less abstract data model as two generic entities in a recursive relationship. In fact a TUAKASUDM is the logical conclusion of allowing either data value differentiated data objects (see Data Value–Differentiated

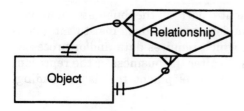

Figure 6.11 Excessive abstraction. This structure can represent any more complex data model.

Entities and Attributes in this chapter) or excessive abstraction. It says that anything might be related to anything given some relationship. Who can argue with that! The problem is that it's just not very expressive or specific, and readers of the data model know nothing more about the subject after reviewing the data model than they did prior to review.

As always, when trying to decide how abstract or concrete to be, apply the logical data modeling principles. Increase the level of abstraction of a model until the next level would decrease the ability of the model to communicate relevant information to a reader.

Many-to-Many Relationships

Allow a many-to-many (M:N) relationship if the relationship does not have any attributes of its own. Although an M:N relationship is a legitimate end-user concept, some modelers insist on "resolving" it during logical data modeling because no major database management system currently supports the concept.

During database design, the M:N relationships have to be converted to two many-to-one relationships with the introduction of a "junction" or "intersection" record or table (Fig. 6.12). Since it must be done eventually, the obvious question to ask is why not convert them during logical data modeling? The answer: because a junction record is an

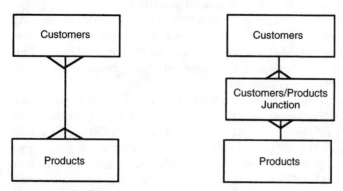

Figure 6.12 A junction or intersection table resolving a many-to-many relationship.

Figure 6.13 An associative entity should not be used to resolve a many-to-many relationship.

artificial construct that hides the end-user fact that a many-to-many relationship exists.

Additionally, "resolving" M:N relationships is a physical design issue that might (or might not) have to be undertaken during database design. After all, who knows what DBMS the database administrators will use or what DBMS will be available in ten years. The logical model should be immune to all physical issues so that the physical designers can separate what is end-user related information from what is relevant to physical design.

If, however, the relationship does have attributes of its own, then an associative entity should be created to store information about the relationship. For example, an automobile has a list price, but it often sells for a totally different amount. The exact price of a car is dependent on who is buying the car and when (Fig. 6.13).

Naming Objects

Data object names should be meaningful yet follow some uniform approach or standard when possible. Avoid naming conventions that aim simply at control, yet fail to communicate. There are only three legitimate reasons to have and enforce a set of naming conventions, namely, to

- Communicate the meaning of a data object.
- Locate a specific data object in a data dictionary.
- Identify similar or related data objects in an application or organization.

However, achieving these objectives is often difficult because

- Data objects usually need multiple names to reflect various tool and/or computer language requirements.
- Most naming conventions in use predate, and are often out of touch with, the current uses of the conventions.

- Uniqueness requirements vary by data object user.
- Naming convention goals vary within an organization.

Each will be examined in turn.

Multiple names

In many cases, an object will need multiple names. Take the logical attribute COMMERCIAL CUSTOMER PRE-TAX CREDIT. This name might be acceptable for the data dictionary and CASE tools, but it is too long for most COBOL compilers. For COBOL you might have to shorten it to, COMM_CUST_PRE_TAX_CREDIT, substituting the underscore for the spaces and the hyphens between the words.

But even this would not be acceptable with many Fortran compilers, which cannot accept more than an eight character name and do not accept an underscore. For such languages, the name might have to be shortened to, TAXCRDT. And even this name may be too long for some assemblers that do not allow names of more than five characters.

The reality is that names are context dependent. What an object is called might need to vary based on the context in which it exists, such as in data dictionaries, CASE tools and computer languages. A context acceptable for the data dictionary might be unacceptable for an APL program.

Naming conventions

Naming conventions are not new. Their use goes back almost to the inception of computer languages. What, then, is new? The many new objects to which naming conventions are applied and the restrictions imposed by the places in which these new objects are stored.

Originally names were limited to identifying physical objects such as files, record types, and fields within record types. To live within the confines of computer languages, system directories, and job cards, a set of rules was established which focused on name restrictions, character length, and the use of delimiters and abbreviations.

Now these same conventions are used to gauge the appropriateness of names for objects, e.g., entities, attributes, relationships, external entities, and much more, which may be stored in a data dictionary or CASE tool. But the old ways of naming objects do not always work well with modern objects or tools. Conventions designed to uniquely define the 20 to 100 data objects in files of yesteryear are inadequate for defining the potentially thousands of data objects in a data dictionary of today. Consequently, names will often need replacement or modification to make sense in the systems organizations of 1990s.

Name uniqueness

All data objects need to be unique within a specific context. But not all tools and languages have the same context. For example:

Maitland Trust Company and Rossetti Marriage Counseling are two separate and unrelated companies. Both have the logical attribute CUSTOMER NAME, but with two different definitions. However, Maitland need not be concerned about Rossetti's name, since the context of the two attributes is very different. Both companies can consider the attribute CUSTOMER NAME unique.

In the same vein, one of Maitland's assembler programs might use the variable CUSTN for "customer name," while another Maitland program uses CUSTN for "custody number." Both are acceptable uses of CUSTN because the context (the program) of the two variables is different.

While the name must be unique within its context, in this case the computer program, the name need not be unique outside its context. In the Maitland example above, there is no confusion even though the programs reuse variable names because the context in which the names are used is different.

Contexts can vary by object. Whereas logical attribute names might have to be unique across the enterprise, relationships need only be unique between entities. For example, it is acceptable to have the relationship entity pairs 'Customers Buy Products' and 'Divisions Buy Raw Materials,' because the entities which tie together the relationship "buy" are unique (Table 6.4).

Naming convention goals

Everyone within an organization does not have the same goals for a set of naming conventions. Two groups often at loggerheads are data

TABLE 6.4   The Context of Uniqueness Can Vary by Object

Object Type	Uniqueness Context
• Attribute	• Enterprise
• Entity	• Enterprise
• Relationship	• Between entities
• Record	• File or database
• Field	• Record
• File	• Database or system
• Database	• Enterprise

TABLE 6.5   Comparison of Data Administration and Application Development Goals

Data Administration Goals	Application Development Goals
• Names unique across enterprise	• Names unique within program, application, database, etc.
• Central control of names and all changes	• Application developer freedom to customize and shorten names
• Names are dictionary-oriented	• Names are tool or programming language-oriented

administration and application development. Projects sometimes suffer because the data administration group sees naming conventions as a means to *control* and *regulate* the collective data asset, while the application developers are concerned with *ease of use, productivity, and building applications in the quickest and cheapest way possible*. Conflict is often unavoidable (Table 6.5)

However, the clash can often be avoided, or at least minimized, with some preproject understanding for the contexts of the different data objects.

Naming conventions should reflect the needs of both groups:

- To facilitate the use of the data objects, while

- Providing a modicum of control.

In some organizations there is often little room for negotiation—with the application developers having to "buckle under" to the prevailing standards. However, if these two groups are viewed as two separate contexts, compromise is possible.

While naming conventions vary, a good context-sensitive naming convention for attributes might look something like the following:

Sample: Context-sensitive attribute logical naming convention

- The name consists of full words—no abbreviations unless necessary. Length should be as long as necessary—60 characters is not excessive.

- Do not use abbreviations unless they are

  Routinely used by a business (see Abbreviations entry).

  Or absolutely necessary for the data object name to fit in the data dictionary.

- Delimiter is a blank, i.e, CUSTOMER NAME not CUSTOMER_ NAME or CUSTOMER-NAME.
- The name should be unique within context.
- The name should be in English.
- The name should follow a consistent naming framework or rule set (see below).
- The name should not contain special characters, codes, prefixes, or suffixes to specify the source, location, organization, entities, technology, or use of the object.
- Names should follow a naming rule set *as much as possible* given tool and data dictionary restrictions.

When creating object names, a set of rules should be applied. A popular rule set is the Prime-Modifier-Class approach.

Sample: Attribute naming rule set

- All attribute names should be constructed of words in a specified order; i.e.,

Prime Word [+ Modifier] + Class Word

Prime Word is a noun used to identify a basic data object, such as Customer, Account, and Employee.

Modifier is an adjective which further describes the prime word, such as Current and Last.

Class Word describes the object classification. Examples would be Address, Amount, Name.

- There should be only one Prime Word and only one Class Word per name.
- A name could have zero to many Modifiers.

An example of a correctly named attribute, using the above framework, would be CUSTOMER LAST NAME. Names should follow these rules *as much as possible*, given tool and dictionary length restrictions.

Physical objects will need a different set of conventions and rule set.

Sample: Context-sensitive physical naming convention

- Maximum length of the name is determined by the tool or computer language used. For example, the length would vary for COBOL, DB2, and Assembler.

- Abbreviations are used where needed to conform with length restrictions.

- Names need not be unique across the entire enterprise, only within context.

- Delimiter is language dependent.

- Names should follow the naming rule set *as much as possible* given the computer language length restrictions. For example, an eight-character assembler language name cannot support the Prime-Modifier-Class construct.

Naming conventions for other data objects, such as entities, relationships, or programs, can be similarly constructed. If the result of using a naming convention is a series of unintelligible phrases, then there is something wrong with the convention, and the phrases should be either changed or replaced.

Rule sets such as the Prime-Modifier-Class set mentioned above can be particularly problematic. Keep rule sets in perspective. Remember:

- Most rule sets will produce junk from time to time.

- Always let reason prevail over form (form follows reason). If the output of a rule set is unintelligible, change the name to something that is reasonable and makes sense—regardless of what the rules say.

Which naming approach you use is less important than achieving some level of agreement as to its purpose. For example, if the data administration and application development team discussions focus on why and where naming conventions are needed, rather than on how they are to be enforced, a satisfactory approach is usually possible. (See Abbreviations entry.)

N-ary Relationships

Relationships can legitimately exist between two, three, or more entities. Many data modeling techniques and the most famous of them all, the Entity-Relationship Approach, support n-ary relationships. However, most CASE tools do not allow greater than binary relationships (Fig. 6.14).

In the real world, however, three-way and more-way relationships certainly exist. For example, take the case of a customer buying a car from a dealer. While this is a legitimate three-way relationship, most CASE tools will require that the relationship be diagrammed

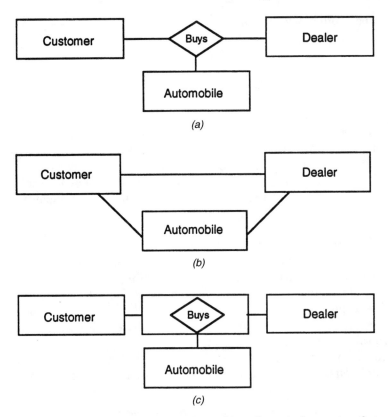

Figure 6.14 Diagramming n-ary relationships. Some tools require that (a) n-ary relationships be represented as (b) three binary relationships or as (c) an "empty" associative entity.

- With two or three separate binary relationships
- Or as an empty associative entity

Neither accurately reflects the business. (See Empty Entities entry.)

While it is true that most CASE tools simply do not support exotic relationships such as exclusion, conjunction, and n-ary relationships, that is not a good excuse for ignoring robust relationships. These relationships are legitimate and valuable end-user concepts that should be documented if they exist. How it is documented could be tool specific. On some tools, the exclusive or n-ary nature of a relationship might have to exist only as comments in the definition of relationships.

Another excuse frequently cited for excluding n-ary relationships is that none of the major DBMSs directly supports them. However, future systems might, and probably will, support these relationships. If their occurrence is not documented, the information will be lost when more sophisticated products become available. Moreover, physical designers could implement n-ary relationships through application code if the need is sufficient.

Normalization

Normalize data models where possible, but do not break any logical data modeling best practices to do so. Normalization is the application of a set of mathematical rules to a database to eliminate or reduce insertion, update, and deletion (IUD) anomalies. It does this by ensuring that all fields are completely dependent on the record key for their existence and not on any other field. Properly applied, normalization can go a long way toward solving the problem of deleting a record that contains one type of data, and in the process, inadvertently deleting other information. (See Chap. 4.)

Though designed to be used on physical databases, the concept works, in whole or in part, for logical data modeling and can improve the viability of the model. In fact, many modelers believe that normalization should be at least started during logical data modeling, since IUD unpleasantries, like most problems, can be more easily nipped in the bud in the early stages of a project.

Normalization is broken down into levels; the higher the level, the more normalized the database. It is somewhat universally agreed that

TABLE 6.6   Differences between E-R Modeling and Normalization

Entity-Relationship Modeling	Normalization
• Entity focused	• Data element (attribute) focused
• Top-down analysis:	• Bottom-up analysis

– Define an entity
  – Populate it with attributes
	– After elements (attributes) have been assigned to record types (entities), ask the question, "Does this data element depend on the record key?"
	
	  – If not, move the element to a new record type

• The question, "Is this attribute in the right entity?" is never asked	• The question, "Is this the right key for this record type?" is never asked

the third level (called Three Normal Form) or the fourth level (called Boyce-Codd Normal Form) is sufficient for most databases, though academics have created seven levels or more.

Unfortunately, some modelers confuse normalization with data modeling and assume that if they follow the rules of normalization, their data model will be correct. This is not true. Whereas the focus of data modeling is on entities and the relationships between them, the focus of normalization (in data modeling terms) is on attributes and the relationships between attributes (Table 6.6).

Logical data modelers (at least those who are not normalization fans) have three complaints about normalization:

- Normalization is a review, not a design, process. It assumes that records (entities) already exist and the question to be answered is, "Is the data element living in the correct record?" This provides little guidance for identifying and modeling new entities and attributes.

- Normalization is a decomposition process. It is a process that breaks down or decomposes existing "compound" records (entities) into simpler ones. However, it does not provide a method of going in the reverse direction; i.e., if the abstraction of the data is too granular, there is no way to build up to a more appropriate level.

- Normalization says little about key suitability. It is concerned with ensuring that only the proper descriptive attributes are in the entity; nothing is said about whether the entity has the proper key. For example, normalization would not flag as an error the key of Employee being PART NUMBER. In fact, it would reject EMPLOYEE NAME from Employee because it is not dependent on PART NUMBER.

Normalization as a logical data modeling technique

The fact that normalization is a physical database design process should not be of concern. In reality, normalization is probably more relevant to logical data modeling than it is to physical database design for three reasons:

- It does not dictate any physical implementation direction.

- The process reduces compound entities—those that house information about more than one thing—into simple, single "thing" entities.

- The performance of a normalized database is traditionally very poor compared to nonnormalized databases, and thus normalized databases are rarely implemented. One of the major functions of many physical database design approaches is to denormalize a model after it has been normalized to improve performance.

The major problem with normalizing in logical data modeling is that to normalize properly, all entities must have at least one identifier. If there is more than one identifier, one of the identifiers must be designated as a prime identifier to correspond to the normalization concept of a primary key.

Nevertheless, normalization, in whole or in part, should be undertaken during logical data modeling—but only to the extent that it can be accomplished without corrupting the logical data modeling process. In practice, however, normalization cannot be completed during logical data modeling. At least some elements of normalization must wait until physical database design. For best results:

- Follow the Entity-Relationship approach *and* normalize.

- Normalize as early as possible—if you can, normalize during analysis.

- However, do not alter the business to follow normalization rules—do not create data objects to satisfy normalization.

In summary, normalization does not replace, nor should it alter, any logical data modeling guidelines. It is simply a database design technique that modelers would be wise to apply to entities and attributes early in the modeling process.

Null Attributes

Null attributes are perfectly acceptable, but they should be scrutinized carefully and dependence on them should be discouraged. (Make sure they are not the result of combining multiple entities or subtypes into one.) The problem surrounding nulls—as primary keys or as attributes—is a recent issue. Originally nulls were only used internally by database management systems to conserve space. When passed to an application program, they were converted to either blanks or zeroes.

Relational systems, or, more appropriately, the interfaces to relational systems such as SQL, have made them widely accessible to the application programmer. For this reason, some people incorrectly assume that nulls are a relational construct.

Ironically, relational systems programmers are the ones who have problems with nulls. Many relational advocates believe that nulls are often misunderstood and/or used improperly, leading to errors in output. To solve the problem, they favor banning their use altogether. (Of course, most people do not know how to fill out their tax returns, yet I know of no expert who suggests banning their use!)

Nulls in primary keys

The argument against nulls in a primary key comes from relational theorists. Their principal spokesperson is author Chris Date. The argument goes as follows:

- Every tuple (relational talk for "record") should have a primary key which is unique.

- The primary key should follow the "minimality" rule; i.e., it should consist of the minimum number of attributes so that if one attribute is removed, the key is no longer unique.

- Therefore, nulls cannot make up part of the primary key since they are not a value, but rather the lack of a value. For a primary key to include a null means that

The minimality rule is broken.

Or the key is no longer unique.

But this whole argument is based on a premise that is tied into relational theory and not logical data modeling. Here is the problem:

- A basic conflict exists between the real world and relational theory. Businesses can have relationships that are more complex than simple binary relationships; however, relational theory can only handle binary relationships.

- Imagine a situation where the relationships among three entities are linked with an *exclusive or*. Entity 'A' can be related to entity 'B' or entity 'C,' but not both. The relationship is exclusive.

- The primary key of 'A' could be a foreign key that is either the primary key of 'B' (call it b) or the primary key of 'C' (call it c), but not both. Expressed as a single value, the primary key would be the concatenation of the attributes b and c, where for any occurrence the value is one or the other, but not both. The nonexpressed value would be null.

- However, the primary key is still unique (Fig. 6.15).

The uniqueness and minimality rules stated earlier might appear to be broken; however, the intention is still intact. And this was done while still representing the business.

Let's take the example of Product, Invoice, and Line Item relations in which the primary key of Product is PRODUCT NUMBER, Invoice INVOICE NUMBER, and Line Item the concatenation of INVOICE NUMBER and PRODUCT NUMBER (Fig. 6.16).

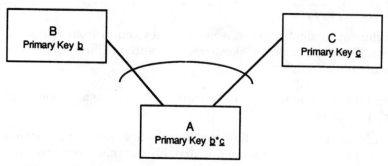

Figure 6.15   Nulls in primary keys.

Let's assume the following business rules also apply:

- A product can appear, at most, as one line item per invoice.
- All line items are for one product except for a discount line item given to all invoices over $1,000.00, for which no product is specified.

In this example, for every discount there is an occurrence of Line Item where the PRODUCT NUMBER attribute (and thus that part of the primary key) is null. This is a legitimate end-user situation and must be modeled accordingly.

How and when the null is resolved is a physical issue, however, and not your concern. For "logical" purposes, the use of null is OK since logical data modeling does not require the identification of a primary key. Applying Date's arguments in this situation is a misapplication of physical design concerns.

Nulls as descriptors

Certain logical designers claim that the frequent use of null values in attributes is a sign of modeling "uncleanness" at best, a grave error at worst. A large number of nulls usually signals that the designer is com-

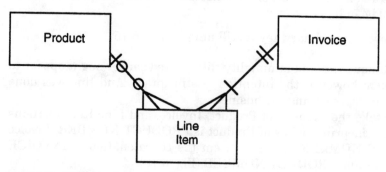

Figure 6.16   Nulls in primary keys.

bining multiple different entity types into one. Splitting the offending entity into many will usually remove the odious nulls.

For example, imagine an Invoice entity that contains the attributes DISCOUNT, MINIMUM ORDER, SALESMAN, and CONTRACT NUMBER for commercial accounts and the attributes CREDIT CARD NUMBER and ORDER SOURCE (i.e., whether the order was from a catalog or phoned in) for retail customers. For a given occurrence, the first four attributes will be null if the customer is retail, while the latter two will be null if the customer is commercial.

To avoid the nulls, split the Invoice entity into two or, even better, three entities as indicated in Fig. 6.17. Now there is no need for nulls.

Note that in this example the relationship between Commercial and Retail and Invoice is an *exclusive or*, i.e., one occurrence of Invoice can associate with one occurrence of Commercial or with one occurrence of Retail, but not both. (See Exclusive Relationships and Supertypes and Subtype entries.)

One last reason given for rejecting nulls is that they change systems based on two-valued logic (true and false) into three-valued logic systems (true, false, null), and current computer languages simply do not handle three-valued logic. While that is true, the problem can be easily resolved since database designers can require that all nulls be stored as either a blank or a zero—abrogating the entire null argument. In any event, the argument is misplaced, since it is a physical design issue not appropriate for logical design.

Optional Relationships (Optional-Optional Relationships)

Allow optional relationships. The argument against optional relationships is usually voiced by relational database theorists who are upset at the possibility of having a null value as part of a key (Fig. 6.18).

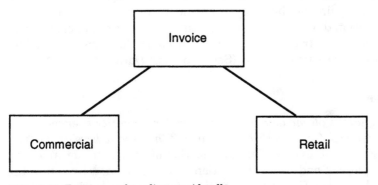

Figure 6.17 Entities can be split to avoid nulls.

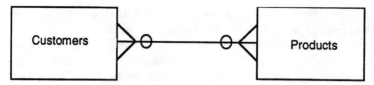

Figure 6.18 Optional relationship.

Contrary to what some relational database advocates believe, optional relationships do not require nulls in primary keys, but nulls are possible if the primary key is also a foreign key (see entries on Null Attributes, Primary Keys, and Foreign Keys). However, since null values and keys are physical design questions, they are not relevant to a discussion of logical data modeling.

Presentation Data

Do not model reports, transactions, screens, or views. Presentation data is not atomic end-user data but rather the replication of atomic, compound, or derived data. An example illustrates this point.

The Flotsam and Jetsam database contains a data element AMOUNT DUE in the Order record. The same element is called DUE on the order entry screen and ITEM AMOUNT in the daily sales input. On the customer order confirmation form AMOUNT DUE is AMOUNT DUE from the order record plus any SHIPPING CHARGE from the shipping record minus any DISCOUNT from the Product record. Only SHIPPING CHARGE, DISCOUNT, and the AMOUNT DUE from Order (probably with a better name) should be on the data model.

The exclusion of presentation data from the model seems obvious, but it can be a problem. The problem can be exacerbated by using one set of data object names for presentation purposes and another for internal uses. Some digging by the analysts should uncover the problem.

Presentation data is really an odd combination of both derived data and nondiscrete attributes. Careful attention to the derivation of data should uncover its true nature. (See Transient Data entry.)

Primary Keys

The designation of one or more identifiers for an entity is encouraged, but not required. The specification of one of the unique keys as the "primary key" is unnecessary. The specification of identifiers for an entity is a good piece of end-user information. If it is known, convey it to the physical designers. However, the notion of a "primary key," or arbitrarily picking an identifier and specifying it as a primary key, is a physical design concern, and not relevant to logical data modeling. The insistence on identifying primary keys is a good sign that the modeler has trouble distinguishing logical from physical data modeling.

What is more important, but also not required, is the identification of identifiers. That an attribute or group of attributes can uniquely identify an entity occurrence is important information that should be communicated back to the user for verification and to physical designers for possible use as a key. If an entity type has multiple identifiers, which one to pick to be the primary key is unimportant, arbitrary, and irrelevant to logical data modeling. (See Identifiers entry.)

Process Data

Do not model process data, data flows, triggers, formulas, policy, rules, or the passing of control. Since process data is not atomic end-user data but rather derived data, transformation data, or internal flags used by an application to control process flow, it should not be modeled. When process data is modeled, it usually reflects one of two problems:

- Regardless of training or warnings, some people will read a data model as a process model, which prompts them to introduce some temporal notions (e.g., how data might look at different times during its life) into the model. In short order, what evolves is a mini dataflow diagram masquerading as a logical data model.

- Some analysts and designers interpret data-driven development to mean that things such as business policy or business rules should be placed in the logical data model. Or they are simply puzzled as to where they should store documented business rules and policy, and lacking an alternative, store them in the data dictionary.

The data model, however, is only for data objects that *can* be modeled.

- Rules and policy which do not fit into the data modeling definition of an attribute or an entity should not be included on the model.

- Though simple single attribute rules, such as a credit limit, can be modeled, "if...then, else" rules cannot be put into the logical data modeling format and should be excluded from the model.

- Textual material, such as a business policy statement that is not interpretable by a computer, should also be excluded. Clearly, the CEO's annual report policy statement is important, but it does not belong on the data model.

- Last, just because something should go into the physical database does not mean it should be modeled. An application development organization might decide to build table-driven systems (applications that use tables to direct computer processing) and to store the tables in the database. This is perfectly appropriate, but the system tables should not be data modeled. They are process data that developers have decided should be performed interpretatively. Simply because they are stored in the database does not mean that they are not processing code.

There is some relevant history that might be of some interest. Data modeling, or at least modern data modeling, was started by Charles Bachman. Bachman Diagrams used boxes for records (entities) and arrows for set (relationships). Two problems quickly became apparent. First, how do you tell the difference between a process model and data model at first blush? Answer: It is not always easy. Second, the Bachman Diagram was also used to represent a database schema (and, with most network database ace management systems, it still is). This confusion with process models and database schema led some to seek a distinct diagramming technique for logical data modeling. The results have been good, but as this entry implies, confusion sometimes still reigns. (See Transient Data entry in this chapter.)

Repeating Groups

Do not allow repeating groups, since they can hide entity and relationship data. Somewhere back in the history of data processing, someone discovered that punch card–based systems could simulate variable numbers of field records by a clever trick. Have the first card contain a field with the integer value of the number of cards to follow. The subsequent cards are then interpreted as a repeating field or group of fields (Fig. 6.19) (see Group Data Items entry).

Using the repeating field concept, programmers did not have to know the maximum number of address fields a customer could have, nor did they have to allocate the large amount of precious memory space to store all of them.

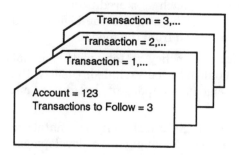

Transaction = 3,...
Transaction = 2,...
Transaction = 1,...
Account = 123
Transactions to Follow = 3

Figure 6.19 Using cards to represent repeating fields.

A repeating field was a very useful concept in the '50s, '60s and even the '70s, but it is totally outdated today and, at the very least, certainly a physical implementation issue that does not belong in logical data modeling. The problem is that a repeating group is in reality not a group but a separate entity in relationship to at least one other entity. For example, the multiple addressses in Customer should be in the separate entity Customer Address with a relationship to Customer and possibly other entitites (Fig. 6.20). If address information is kept in the Customer entity, this relationship information is lost.

Subject Areas

Allow subject areas. Subject areas partition the data model into smaller parts. But, the model should be segmented in a way that minimizes cross-subject-area relationships. For example, a banking data model might be partitioned into two subject areas for customer related entities and account related entities. This segmentation reduces the number of relationships that are required to span the partition.

Subject areas are also a good way to partition a data model for tasking purposes (dividing a data modeling exercise up into separate smaller pieces so that multiple individuals or teams can work simultaneously without stepping on each other's toes).

They are also used, though with less success, as a means of breaking a big data model down into multiple physical databases. The reason subject areas are a poor method of database design is because subject areas do not take into account how the data will be used. For example, to say that there should be a customer database and an invoice database is acceptable if an application has no need to access both customer and invoice information. However, if you need customer and invoice information together, you might want to store them in the same database. But, you obtain this information from the process model, not from the data model. The data model only gives information on the relationship

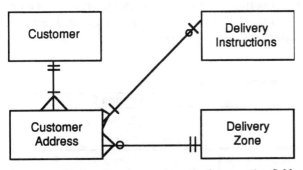

Figure 6.20 Designating a separate entity for repeating fields.

between data, not how data should be physically stored. To develop a physical database design solely on logical data is a serious mistake.

There is a second danger to guard against when using subject areas. The subject area can become a self-fulfilling prophecy. The subject areas at the beginning of the data modeling process might not be the ones you should have at the end. Unless the modeler is careful, early subject areas could become permanent unless the modelers constantly review and correct the structure.

Another word of caution. Do not confuse subject databases with subject areas (Table 6.7). The first is a physical design issue involving physical constraints based on how data is accessed, while the second is a logical data modeling construct based on entity relationships involved with the issues of clarity or tasking. The reason to have multiple databases instead of one is usually driven by the physical size of the database, transaction volume, and/or location.

Substitution Data

Do not model substitution data unless it is necessary for understanding the business. Substitution data is usually located in an abbreviation table that allows the storage of smaller information in large occurrence record types. For example, for a customer database, the physical designers might decide to store only postal codes, such as ZIP codes, with the customer information. When data is to be accessed, a conversion table is read to fetch the name of the town relating to the postal code. The user will see both the elements POSTAL CODE and TOWN NAME, although only the former is stored with other customer information.

Substitution tables can include such things as state codes (NJ = New Jersey), abbreviations (A = Active, I = Inactive) or transaction codes (07 = Add Customer). When to use substitution data is a physical performance issue best left to physical database designers.

Substitution data, in general, is a physical design issue and should not be part of the data model unless its exclusion will decrease the clarity of the model. Whereas postal codes can easily be excluded, certain product names and product codes should be included.

TABLE 6.7   Subject Areas vs. Subject Databases

Concept	Segmentation Criteria
• Subject Area	• Relationships between Entities
• Subject Database	• Data Access

Supertypes and Subtypes

The use of supertypes and subtypes is acceptable. Supertypes and subtypes (S-types to the *in* crowd) are useful to show how an entity can fulfill multiple roles involving different attribute types. As an approach for avoiding null attributes without having to duplicate relationships, they are particularly useful. The point to remember about an S-type is that it does not represent multiple entities with multiple relationships, but rather it is a single entity that plays many roles. A subtype represents each role that has its own attributes. The attribute types common across all roles are part of the supertype. Subtypes inherit the attributes of the supertype (Fig. 6.21).

Some modelers prefer to have all relationships to the S-types linked through the supertype, but this is only appropriate for relationships that are common for all roles (Fig. 6.22). As with attributes, subtypes inherit the relationships of the supertype.

Some relationships only apply to one or a few roles. These relationships should be represented through the subtype (Fig. 6.23). Linking these relationships through the supertype would hide important information about how the role relates to other entities.

In the above example, Products and Orders relate to Customers, while Salesman only relates to the Commercial role of a Customer. The Federal Systems Division entity is linked only to Government Customers.

Note: S-types sometimes go under the name of Generalization or Specialization.

Transient Data

Do not model transient data, since it is usually temporary, duplicate, or process-related data. This concept is best introduced through an example. Imagine an application that uses a memo post approach to update a database; i.e., changes are taken online during the day and written to a transaction file. At night, a batch program reads the transaction file

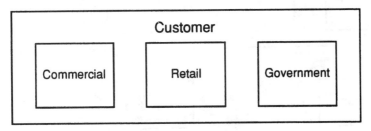

Figure 6.21   A nested supertype.

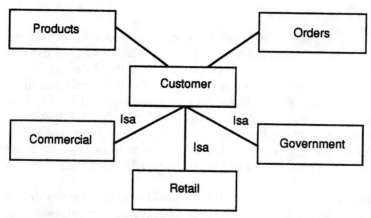

Figure 6.22 Subtype relationships through the supertype. All common relationships are through the supertype.

and updates the database. The question is, "Should the transaction file be modeled?" The answer is, in most cases, "No," for two reasons. First, the data in the transaction file is duplicate data. To model it would mean that attributes, such as CUSTOMER NAME, would appear in both the Customer and Transaction entities. Second, the transaction file has a very limited life and therefore should be looked upon, in process modeling terms, as a very slow data flow rather than as a data store (Fig. 6.24).

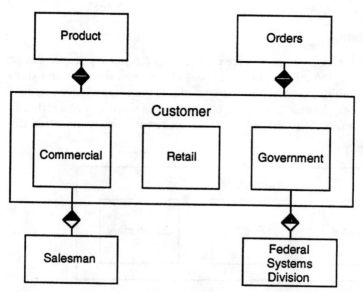

Figure 6.23 Common relationships are through the supertype and role relationships through the subtype.

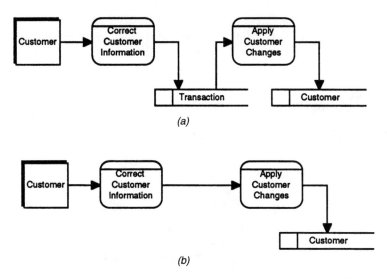

Figure 6.24 Transaction file viewed as (a) a data store and (b) a data flow.

The single exception to this rule is when the exclusion of transaction data causes considerable business data or business process loss or differences. In that case, include it in the model.

Location dependent data

Location dependent data is an interesting variation of the transient data problem. Years ago, when information was stored on ledger cards, data was separated into batches by its status. Active accounts might be located in one "tub" (special cabinets to handle large numbers of ledger cards) and inactive accounts in another. The status of an account was determined by the tub in which the card was located.

Early electronic systems continued this practice. First, punch cards came in various colors corresponding to the tub file in which they were located. Active accounts might be in the blue tub (and have blue punch cards), inactive accounts in the green tub, and accounts containing some error in the red suspense tub.

Tubs eventually became disk files, and the rest, as they say, is history—unfortunately. There are still systems being built that use the location of the record, whether it is in the master, suspense, or transaction file, to determine the status of the record.

For modeling purposes, the location of an entity is not a property of the entity. Status, such as active, inactive, or suspense, is a value of one or more attributes—not a location on disks, in tubs, or whatever. In logical data modeling, an account is not moved to an inactive file—it is declared "inactive."

Transient data can appear as presentation data, transaction data, suspense data, location dependent data, process data, temporary data, in-process data, transformation data or what have you. If it is transient, do not model it.

Relationship of Guidelines to Principles

All the guidelines relate to a data modeling principle:

- Communication Principle

    - Abbreviations
    - Clarity
    - Conceptual Integrity
    - Data Values
    - Data Value Differentiated Entities and Attributes
    - Extraneous Relationships
    - Level of Abstraction
    - Naming Objects
    - Subject Areas
    - Substitution Data

- Granularity Principle

    - Conceptual Integrity
    - Derived Data
    - Discrete Attributes
    - Embedded Attributes
    - Empty Entities
    - Group Data Items
    - Normalization
    - Presentation Data
    - Process Data
    - Repeating Groups
    - Transient Data

- Logical Representation Principle

    - Compound Identifiers
    - Conjunctive Relationships
    - Exclusive Relationships
    - Foreign Keys
    - Identifiers
    - Many-to-Many Relationships
    - N-ary Relationships
    - Null Attributes
    - Optional Relationships
    - Primary Keys
    - Supertypes and Subtypes

7

Rules of Thumb

*"Entia non sunt multiplicanda paveter
necessitatem"—"Entities should not be
multiplied beyond necessity."*   OCKHAM

*"I learned an awful lot from him by doing the
opposite."*   HOWARD HAWKES

The leap from logical data modeling guidelines to rules of thumb is relatively subtle. Rules of thumb should be looked upon as checkpoint guidelines. Sometimes they tell the modeler something is wrong; other times they signal that a specific situation is fertile ground for further investigation. While they are useful for building a model, they are especially useful when the modeler is called upon to assess an existing data model or a data model under construction.

This chapter does not present standards or principles. Rather, what follows are data modeling "situations" that frequently—but not always—point out a data modeling error or misrepresentation. The rules of thumb, taken with the principles presented in Chap. 2 and the guidelines in the previous chapter, form a set of logical data modeling best practices. And, as with the guidelines, the reader should bear in mind that not all the rules of thumb will apply to both the end-user and detailed logical data models; those that do apply to both do not always do so equally (Table 7.1).

"Almost Unique" Identifiers

Identify "almost unique" identifiers when known, since they can be useful for application development. Ideally there are unique and nonunique attributes. But the world is not as clean and simple as this. Sometimes there are attributes that might not be mathematically

TABLE 7.1 Applying Rules of Thumb to Data Models

Rules of Thumb	End-User Model	Detailed Model
"Almost Unique" Identifiers		√
Associative Related to Other Associatives		√
Circular Relationships	√	√
Diagrammable Objects	√	√
Disassociated Entity Clusters ("Islands")		√
Duplicate Identifiers		√
Duplicate Subtype/Supertype "Type" Data		√
Entity Fragmentation		√
Junction Entities	√	√
Multiple Relationships	√	√
One of a Kind (OOAK) Entities	√	√
One-to-One Relationships		√
Rare Entity Relationships	√	√
Recursive Relationships, Cardinality, and Modality	√	√
Single Attribute Entities		√
"Spiderwebs"		√
Substitution Tables		√
Symmetrical Models, Relationships, Attributes		√
Too Many Nulls		√
Too Many Recursives	√	√

Note: √ Indicates to which model a rule of thumb applies. Not all rules of thumb apply to both data models.

unique, but they are sufficiently unique to be useful. Examples include people's names, employee or student numbers that are reissued after a period of time, and even social security numbers (occasionally an SSN is mistakenly issued to more than one person).

Almost unique attributes have varying levels of uniqueness. Names might be much less unique than reissued employee numbers. Whereas a not completely unique employee number might be acceptable as a record key in a database, a name probably would not. But a person's name is sufficiently unique to serve as an adequate secondary index.

Many magazine publishers use a "match code" consisting of a string of nonunique attributes which, when put together, form a key that is very close to being unique for even very large populations.

Example: Magazine match code

Characters   1–5   First five digits of Postal Code

6–10 First five characters of last name

11–11 First name initial

12–14 First three digits of street number

15–18 First four characters of street name

19–20 Tie breaker

A second type of almost unique identifier is an attribute which is unique for only a part of its life. Imagine an organization which reuses document numbers after a maximum number is reached, but never before 2 years have expired. For example, let's asssume the maximum document number is 99,999, but it will take, on the average, 4 years to reach that number. The database designer should feel comfortable that the document number will be unique for at least a while, but after that period caution is needed.

Almost unique identifier information is useful for physical designers and should be communicated to them.

Associatives Related to Other Associatives

Be wary of associatives related to other associatives, since in a correct model they are somewhat rare. When an associative related to another associative correctly occurs, it is usually in the form of an event related to another event. Let's take the following case:

The purchasing department employees of Chatterton Enterprises are classified as one of several types of corporate purchasing agents. The associative entity Job is time dependent, i.e., an Employee could function in many Departments over his or her career. When an Employee is in the purchasing department, he/she can, but not always will, function as a purchasing agent—also a time dependent position. The diagram would look like that in Fig. 7.1.

Although the above is legitimate, the use of associatives related to associatives is not that common. Therefore, when you see associatives related to associatives on a logical data model, review them closely. The odds are in favor of their being incorrect.

Circular Relationships

Circular relationships are impossible. A circular relationship is the data modeling equivalent of a cat chasing its tail. If you have a circular

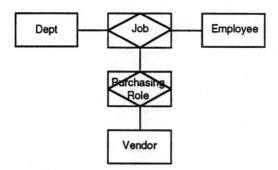

Figure 7.1 Associative related to another associative.

relationship, then at least one relationship and/or one entity is wrong. To prove this to yourself, try to construct one. You will quickly see that the task leads to a meaningless model (Fig. 7.2).

The problem might be that a one-to-many relationship is actually a one-to-one or many-to-many relationship, or that one of the entities should be two entities or part of another entity.

Diagrammable Objects

Not all data objects should be represented on the diagram of the logical data model. Carefully review all data objects to determine which ones should be part of the model. When modelers talk about data objects, they mean two different types of data:

- Data objects which are candidates for being on a logical data model

  Entities

  Relationships

  Primitive attributes (For space reasons attributes are usually not on the diagram but are represented by the entity in which they participate)

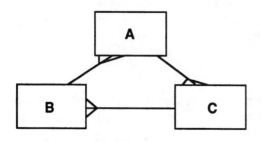

Figure 7.2 (Meaningless) circular relationships.

- Valid data objects which should be in the data dictionary but should not be on the logical data model diagram or listed as part of an entity on the diagram

  Global data

  Derived data

  Transient data

  Presentation data (screen or report data)

All data objects need to be documented and placed in a data dictionary (whether it be an automated dictionary or a loose-leaf binder). However, only certain primitive data is placed in the logical data model.

A clear understanding should be reached by all on the development team about which objects are diagrammed and documented and which are only documented. The data administration group should handle global data, such as CURRENT DATE. Application-specific attributes such as NEXT ACCOUNT NUMBER and NEXT BILLING DATE need to be documented by the application development team and the data stored in the data dictionary, but the attributes are usually not placed on the data model diagram.

Derived data is actually a process and should be documented in the process model.

Do not model presentation data. Rather presentation data should exist in the data dictionary if it is different from its source (the diagrammed data it represents).

Transient data is process specific and should be documented in the process model.

Disassociated Entity Clusters ("Islands")

Since legitimate disassociated entities and entity clusters are rare, their occurrence on the model most often reflects incorrectly modeled data. Data models have entities that are related to other entities. A few data models, however, may have entities that are not related to any other entities. These entities generally are referred to as disassociated entities and sometimes called "islands." A small group of entities can also function as an island if it is not related to the main body of entities (Fig. 7.3).

The legitimate cases are more common in strongly diversified organizations or are found on a data model which only represents parts of an organization and those parts are weakly related. For example, the data model for a conglomerate that sells services to the government and commercial products to consumers might have a disjointed data model. Also, a data model that is limited to raw materials management and stock holder services would also be legitimately disjointed (though one wonders about the application this data model is to support).

Other than the above, entity "islands" are rare. When they do show up they are often incorrectly modeled transient or substitution data. (See Substitution Tables in this chapter and the Transient Data and Substitution Data entries in Chapter 6.)

Duplicate Identifiers

Although it is not uncommon or wrong for two entities to share an attribute as their identifiers, the practice should be discouraged. Ideally, every entity will have an identifier. However the identifier of some entities could be (in whole or in part) the identifier of another entity. Take the example of an Employee subject area (Fig. 7.4).

Each of the entities has an identifier that is in whole or in part the attribute EMPLOYEE NUMBER. However, the better solution is to make the three entities attributive entities and eliminate the duplicate data.

Duplicate Subtype/Supertype "Type" Data

A duplicate "type" attribute is appropriate in subtype/supertype entities. Common attributes should exist in the supertype. Only specific attributes should be in the subtype/supertypes—with one exception.

Many modelers use a special attribute to distinguish the different subtypes. Let's look at an example:

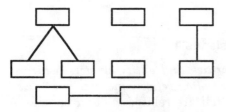

Figure 7.3 Disassociated entity clusters.

Figure 7.4 Duplicate identifiers.

Cooper Parachutes Inc. is developing a data model for their new human resource system. The model must reflect the special attributes and relationships for the four roles of employee: active, retired, terminated, and leave of absence (Fig. 7.5).

To distinguish the roles, Cooper modelers created the EMPLOYEE TYPE attribute with the acceptable values of "Active," "Retired," "Leave of Absence," and "Terminated." To work properly, the modelers must duplicate the attribute EMPLOYEE TYPE in all four subtypes.

This duplication of EMPLOYEE TYPE in all the subtypes is acceptable.

Exclusive and nonexclusive generalization

Many modelers like to use a type or role attribute to differentiate the roles that subtypes play in the supertype. For example, below (Fig. 7.6) is the entity Customer which has two subtypes—Retail and Wholesale. To communicate this information, the modeler created the attribute CUSTOMER TYPE with the acceptable values of "Retail" and "Wholesale."

The important question is whether the role for a subtype in a generalization is best described by an attribute or by a relationship.

Those who use the "Isa" construct (Fig. 7.7), where the subtype is shown in a one-to-one relationship with the supertype, tend to prefer describing the role as a relationship. They would define the role options of retail or wholesale in the relationship definition.

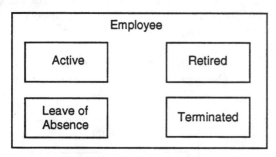

Figure 7.5 Duplicate atttribute data can exist in the subtype.

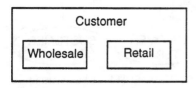

Figure 7.6 Supertype box construct.

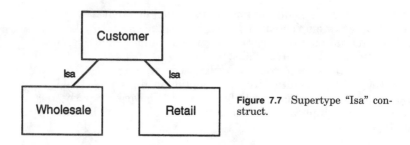

Figure 7.7 Supertype "Isa" construct.

A more popular and probably better approach is to define the subtype role with a type or role attribute such as CUSTOMER TYPE with the acceptable values of "Wholesale" and "Retail." Advocates of this approach prefer that because most subtype roles have a domain of acceptable values, and domains are a property of an attribute, not a relationship. However, this raises another question: Should the type attribute be in the supertype or the subtype? The answer is not always obvious. Let's examine it.

Most modelers place the type attribute in the supertype. Their argument is simple: if you placed the type attribute in the subtype, then the type attribute would have to be duplicated as many times as there are subtypes. Placing the type attribute in the supertype avoids this duplication (Fig. 7.8).

Certainly with the Customer example this would seem to be a good idea. However, this answer assumes that all the roles in which the supertype can participate are exclusive, i.e., if a customer is retail, they are not wholesale and *vice versa*. However, if a supertype occurrence can have more than one role, then the type attribute in the supertype runs into trouble.

Imagine the supertype Soldier with Officer and Enlisted as the two subtypes, MILITARY STATUS as the type attribute, and "Officer" and

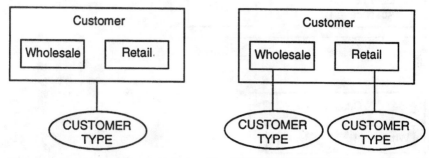

Figure 7.8 Supertype/subtype attributes: Should CUSTOMER TYPE be an attribute of the supertype or the subtype?

"Enlisted" as the acceptable values (Fig. 7.9). While in most cases a soldier is either an officer or enlisted but not both, this is not always the case. There are examples where a soldier is an officer in the reserves but an enlisted person on active duty. For this individual, the supertype occurrence would have both roles and would have to be linked to both subtypes.

If the type attribute MILITARY STATUS is in the supertype, then the acceptable values of the attribute would have to be "Officer," "Enlisted," and "Both." However, if MILITARY STATUS were in the subtype, then the acceptable values could be limited to just "Officer" and "Enlisted."

The military example has only two subtypes. Imagine a case where there are 4, 5, or 10 subtypes. The combinations or nonexclusive supertype participation are quite large and unwieldy. Certainly in these cases, the type attribute works better in the subtype.

The difference between the two cases is that in the first, the subtypes were exclusive—a supertype occurrence could participate in one role, or the other, but not both. In the second case, the roles were not exclusive—a supertype occurrence could participate in one role, the other, or both.

The moral of the story is: unless you are very sure that the generalization is exclusive, it is best to put the type attributes in the subtype.

Required and nonrequired participation

Some supertype occurrences must participate in a subtype as in the Customer and Soldier examples. In other cases supertype participation in a subtype might be optional. Take the case of the supertype Boat with subtypes Sailing and Power Plant used to describe the type of sails it has (if it has any) and/or its engine or engines (also if it has

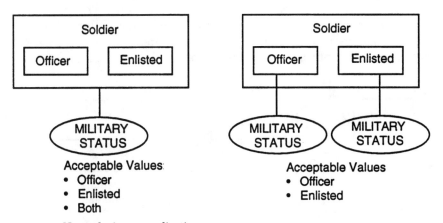

Figure 7.9   Nonexclusive generalization.

any). However, a rowboat has neither sails nor a power plant, so it would not participate in any of these subtypes. Boat would be a supertype which is not required to have a subtype. If the type attribute BOAT TYPE were in the supertype, it would have a value of null or blank. (See also Supertypes and Subtypes in Chap. 6.)

Entity Fragmentation

Avoid unnecessarily fragmenting entities. Some modelers fragment entities into multiple entity types to avoid unnecessary duplication of empty attributes. In Fig. 7.10, the modelers removed TERMINATION DATE from the Employee entity and created a new Termination Date entity, since most employees do not have a TERMINATION DATE. However, the fragmented data can and should be bundled in the subject entity so that TERMINATION DATE along with DATE OF BIRTH and FORMER NAME are all part of Employee. Fragmenting entities just to avoid empty attributes should be discouraged.

Multiple entities, however, are often needed to express information about major business concepts. For example, a logical data model might have a number of entities dealing with a customer or a product. This is one of the reasons for subject areas. However, you must guard against indiscriminately splitting entities, especially for physical reasons, such as to avoid unnecessary empty or null attributes.

Junction Entities

The use of junction records should not be confused with the role of legitimate associative entities. As noted earlier, most physical database management systems do not support many-to-many relationships. For those products, the M:N entity relationships must be "resolved" into two many-to-one physical record type relationships. The resolution often requires an additional record type, sometimes called a junction or intersection record (Fig. 7.11). This is appropriate for physical database design but inappropriate for logical data modeling.

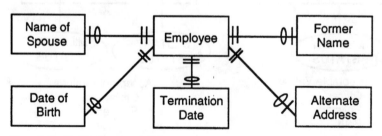

Figure 7.10 Entity fragmentation.

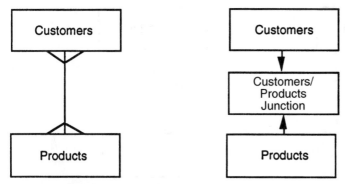

Figure 7.11 Resolving many-to-many relationships. Most DBMSs do not support many-to-many relationships. However, a junction record may be added to "resolve" the many-to-many into two one-to-many relationships.

Associative entities should be viewed as attributed relationships. Unfortunately, many modelers incorrectly believe that at least one of the roles of an associative is to "resolve" a many-to-many relationship. In reality, many-to-many relationships can and should be represented if that is how the data exists in the organization. Do not unnecessarily resolve many-to-many relationships. When reviewing a logical data model, the modeler must ensure that the associatives are attributed relationships and not "resolved" many-to-many relationships.

Multiple Relationships

If more than two or three relationships exist between two entities, you may want to show only one relationship and describe in the relationship definition all the possible relationships. Multiple relationships raise a presentation issue. With some diagrams, displaying excessive relationships between the same two entities can be confusing. If that is the case, show only one or some of the relationships (Fig. 7.12). *Note:* Showing only one or some relationships does not necessarily mean that the other relationships do not exist. Rather, it only reflects that a decision was made not to graphically display the other relationships.

Compressing multiple relationships into one is not required, merely allowed.

One of a Kind (OOAK) Entities

Try to avoid modeling OOAKs. A "One of a Kind" entity, sometimes called an OOAK (rhymes with "nuke") is an entity with a single occurrence. An example of an OOAK would be an entity occurrence that stores the current date, the next account number to assign, or the next

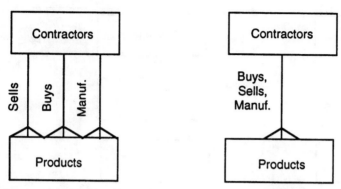

Figure 7.12   Multiple relationships can sometimes be simplified.

billing date. This data goes under various names such as "system data" or "global variable," but it all boils down to the same thing—physical implementation data.

The name OOAK comes from CODASYL DBMS users who use this construct to support global data. By having a single occurrence record type, the necessary data is stored once and is available to all application programs. Since this specifically relates to a physical construct, it should be left out of logical data modeling.

That does not mean that legitimate single occurrence entities will never occur—it just means that they are very, very rare.

One-to-One Relationships

One-to-one relationships, while legitimate, are quite rare. When a one-to-one relationship occurs, usually one of the entity types is part of the other or is a role of the other (subtype/supertype). If a customer can have only one current address, then the Current Address information should be part of the Customer entity (Fig. 7.13).

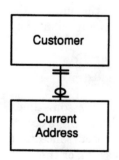

Figure 7.13   One-to-one relationship.

Sometimes a second entity is created to avoid null attributes. Take the example of a financial institution that has a Customer entity consisting of the standard attributes such as CUSTOMER NAME and CUSTOMER ADDRESS. However, 2 percent of its customers are foreign nationals living abroad. For these customers, the firm must store information about their U.S. tax status, both foreign and U.S. addresses, their nationality, etc. To accomplish this, the modelers created a second entity called Foreign Customer Information (Fig. 7.14). The reasons for creating the second entity were as follows:

- If foreign customer information was in the Customer entity, then 98 percent of the Customer occurrences would have null or empty attributes.

- Storing foreign customer information in the Customer entity would waste a considerable amount of space.

Both reasons are, of course, inappropriate. Null or empty attributes are not improper. If the attributes in question are properties of the Customer entity, then they should be in Customer, not somewhere else. Second, computer storage considerations are a physical design issue, and not part of logical data modeling. (See Entity Fragmentation in this chapter.)

Rare Entity Relationships

Certain entity/relationships simply do not occur that often. When they appear on the model, they should be investigated. Rare relationships are usually a sign of poor modeling techniques. Examples are mandatory one-to-one relationships and mandatory many-to-many relationships. Mandatory one-to-one relationships are usually two fragmented entities (see Entity Fragmentation entry in this chapter) that should be a single entity. Mandatory many-to-many relationships are quite rare. When you encounter them, they generally indicate a poor understanding of modality by the model author (Fig. 7.15).

Note: There is nothing wrong with having a mandatory M:N relationship. However, they do not often occur in the real world and are worth a second look by an observant data modeler.

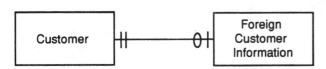

Figure 7.14   Creating a second entity to avoid null values.

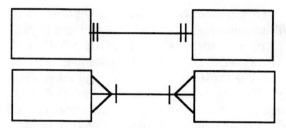

Figure 7.15   Mandatory many-to-many relationships.

Recursive Relationships, Cardinality and Modality

Double-check all recursive relationships, since they are the most likely to be incorrectly modeled. Specifically, check for incorrect modality and cardinality. The cardinality and modality of recursive relationships are determined by the relationship type.

- Asymmetrical relationships cannot be mandatory. If they were, that would mean they fall into an infinite regress.
- Symmetrical relationships can be mandatory-mandatory or optional-optional, but not mandatory-optional or optional-mandatory. The latter two categories are meaningless.
- Symmetrical relationships cannot be one-to-many. One-to-many symmetrical relationships are meaningless.

As was mentioned in Chap. 3, a unary relationship is one in which an association exists between two separate occurrences of the same entity type. For example, the entity Person can be linked to another occurrence of Person by the relationship 'Marries.' This is sometimes called a recursive or reflexive relationship (Fig. 7.16).

A major use of the recursive relationship is to represent a parts or bill of materials structure. Imagine a parts data model with each part consisting of components that are themselves parts, which are made up of other parts, etc. If you know the number of levels, then you can create a structure reflecting these levels (Fig. 7.17).

However, you do not always know the exact number of levels, or the number of levels might change based on the occurrences in the relation-

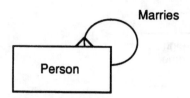

Figure 7.16   A recursive or reflexive relationship.

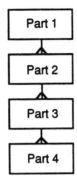

Figure 7.17   A hierarchical structure.

ship. The recursive structure represents a hierarchical structure of any number of levels, or expressed more appropriately, of n levels (Fig. 7.18).

What would be the cardinality and modality of this relationship? The answer, to a certain extent, depends on whether the recursive relationship is symmetrical or asymmetrical.

The 'Succeeds' relationship in the mayor example (Chap. 4) is asymmetrical since the first mayor had no predecessor and the very last mayor has no successor. (The same is at least temporarily true for the current mayor.) To say that every mayor has a predecessor means that there must be an infinite number of mayors stretching back in time forever, which is obviously impossible. Since a mandatory relationship is impossible, the relationship must be optional (Fig. 7.19).

Symmetrical relationships are bi-directional, meaning that if entity 'A' bears some relationship to entity 'B,' then 'B' has the same relationship with 'A.' 'Marries,' 'Dances with,' and 'Dates' are all symmetrical relationships. Asymmetrical relationships are unidirectional, such as 'Hits' and 'Hates' where 'A' may hate 'B,' but that does not mean that 'B' hates 'A.'

The 'Is a Partner of' relationship of the police department example presented in Chap. 4 is a one-to-one recursive relationship that is clearly mandatory and symmetrical (Fig. 7.20).

You can also construct a mandatory recursive many-to-many relationship. In Fig. 7.21, everyone is directly related (parent or sibling) to at least one other person and probably more (actually at least two people since everyone has two parents). This relationship is clearly mandatory. The conclusion is that symmetrical relationships cannot be mandatory, while asymmetrical relationships can be.

However, there are no one-to-many symmetrical relationships. You can test this by trying to convert 'Is a Partner of' to include a police officer's former partners. A police officer must have one and only one partner at a time, but they can change partners as they like. Is this represented in Fig. 7.22? The answer is "No."

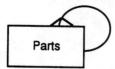

Figure 7.18 A hierarchical structure of n levels.

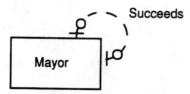

Figure 7.19 An asymmetrical recursive relationship.

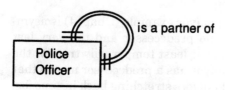

Figure 7.20 A mandatory and symmetrical one-to-one recursive relationship.

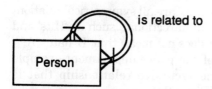

Figure 7.21 A mandatory and symmetrical many-to-many recursive relationship.

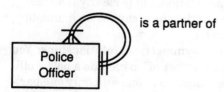

Figure 7.22 A one-to-many symmetrical relationship is impossible.

Let's look at a police officer occurrence (we can call him Officer Molloy). Molloy can have only one partner at a time, but over his career he might have many partners. Is this one-to-many? No, because many officers could have had Molloy as a partner. Actually, the relationship is many-to-many. In reality, a one-to-many symmetrical relationship does not exist (Table 7.2).

Single Attribute Entities

An entity should have more than one attribute in it. Single attribute entities are usually a sign that

- The model is incomplete—the modelers simply have not yet identified all the objects.

- Or, the entity is actually a separate view of an already identified entity.

The first case is straightforward—the modelers simply have not completed the model. Although the entity is understood, its attributes require additional work. Often this is the case when data modeling is performed before process modeling, and the interviewees "ran out of steam" looking for data. Once process modeling gets underway, the additional attributes can be identified.

The second case, however, may signal that entity information resides in more than one entity. Let's look at the example in Fig. 7.23. Both Customer Status and Credit Status each contain only one attribute:

TABLE 7.2   Evaluating Possible Relationships

Cardinality	Modality	Asymmetrical Relationship	Symmetrical Relationship
One-to-One	Mandatory-Mandatory	X	OK
	Optional-Optional	OK	OK
	Mandatory-Optional	X	X
One-to-Many	Mandatory-Mandatory	X	X
	Optional-Optional	OK	X
	Mandatory-Optional	X	X
	Optional-Mandatory	X	X
Many-to-Many	Mandatory-Mandatory	X	OK
	Optional-Optional	OK	OK
	Mandatory-Optional	X	X

Legend: X = Relationship is impossible   OK = Relationship is possible

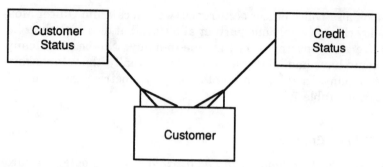

Figure 7.23 Entity information in more than one entity.

- Customer Status contains the CUSTOMER STATUS INDICATOR attribute.

- Credit Status contains only the CREDIT STATUS INDICATOR attribute.

The error is that both attributes should probably be in the Customer entity.

Inexperience is a common cause of this problem. Some modelers incorrectly apply physical database design techniques to a logical data model. For example, they might attempt to facilitate rapid access to certain types of status holders by placing the information in a separate record type.

There is one case when single attribute entities are acceptable, and that is when the entity is associative. Take the case of a library that cares to know who checked out what book and when. *Who* and the *book* are in the entities Borrower and Book. *When* is the only attribute in the associative Borrows (Fig. 7.24).

However, even with associatives, single attribute entities are rare—and should be examined closely.

"Spiderwebs"

"Spiderwebs" are usually the sign of an immature data model or incorrectly defined relationships. Also called "porcupines" or "pin cushions,"

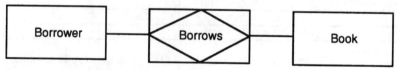

Figure 7.24 Acceptable single attribute entity.

spiderwebs are entities that are directly related to most other entities on the diagram.

Many models will have one or more crucial entities, sometimes called "anchor entities," that form the center of major portions of the diagram (Fig. 7.25). Customer, Account, Product, and Project are excellent candidates for becoming anchor entities.

A data model for a bank could conceivably have a dozen relationships involving Account. That is not wrong. What might be wrong is the linking of all or most entities directly to the anchor, since anchors are usually linked only indirectly (through other entities) to the rest of the model (Fig. 7.26). If you find a spiderweb on a diagram, it is probably

- Incorrectly modeled data.
- Or a simplistic representation of the business.
- Or both.

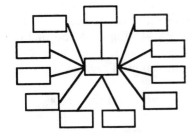

Figure 7.25 A spiderweb data model.

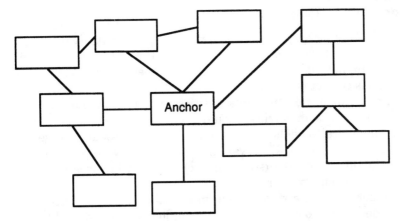

Figure 7.26 An anchor entity forms the core of the data model.

Substitution Tables

Avoid linking substitution tables to other entities. As a rule, do not model substitution data. However, recognize that this is not always practical. There are times when substitution data is essential to the business or when its exclusion detracts from the clarity of the model. In these cases, it should be modeled. *Note*: One of the few instances when disassociated entities (islands) are acceptable is when a substitution table must be modeled. (See Disassociated Entity Clusters in this chapter.)

A substitution table is a list of abbreviations or code definitions that are substituted for the values of the attributes in other entities. For example, the Customer entity might have the attribute POSTAL CODE but not the attribute CITY. Rather, the application goes to a Postal Code/City entity to look up the city name. If the POSTAL CODE in Customer is "08008," then that value is used to find the CITY and STATE values "Ship Bottom, NJ" in the Postal Code/City entity. It would be a mistake to link Customer with Postal Code/City, since their only connection is through a substitution function, not through a business function.

Some modelers do not model substitution tables at all, since they consider their inclusion a strategy to reduce required storage. They view substitution tables as a physical design issue, best left to database designers. Other modelers disagree, stating that the inclusion or exclusion of a substitution table is a business decision, and only if the business does not have them and technical staff creates them is it a physical design issue.

Both approaches have knowledgeable supporters, so the decision of whether to include or exclude them is left up to the individual designer. Either approach is acceptable with the proper justification.

Symmetrical Models, Relationships, Attributes

Be on the lookout for symmetrical models, since they probably represent an incorrect or immature data model. Despite the fact that symmetrical models are not intrinsically wrong, the number of times a symmetrical model is correct is almost zero.

A symmetrical model diagrams entities and relationships so that they line up in a symmetrical (usually mirror image) fashion (Fig. 7.27). Symmetrical models are not uncommon in the early stages of data model development. However, after the first few days the model should take on a more realistic characteristic that involves relationships of a more nonsymmetrical nature.

You cannot say that a symmetrical model is incorrect, because they probably do occur. However, if you see one, look closer—the odds are that you will find errors which destroy the symmetry of the diagram.

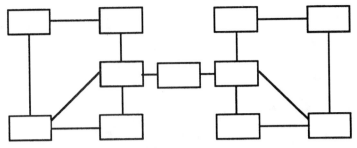

Figure 7.27   Symmetrical model.

Too Many Nulls

Be careful of too many nulls in an entity. They might indicate incorrectly defined entities. Nulls are a cause of concern for many users of some (particularly relational) database management systems. The reason for the concern is that nulls can play havoc with DBMSs which require that all record occurrences have unique keys.

However, in logical data modeling, identifiers, though encouraged, are not required. Nevertheless, an excessive number of nulls can point to another problem—the combining of two separate, though possibly related, "things" into a single entity. (See the Null Attributes entry in Chap. 6.)

Too Many Recursives

Be careful of too many recursive relationships, which often reflect the efforts of an inexperienced data modeler. In a complete detailed data model, you will rarely find more than 2 percent of the relationships diagrammed as recursive relationships. If you do, you probably have surfaced a problem.

Since this problem is not common, there is little data available describing how it comes about, though the most likely cause is "student disease." Student disease is a phenomenon predominantly related to medical and psychology students. It works this way: after hearing about a new disease in class, a number of students are positive that they suffer from the recently discovered malady.

If you find, or have developed, a data model where more than 5 to 10 percent of the relationships are recursive,

- Review the definition and uses of recursives.
- Revisit the data and discuss it with the end users to resolve any misconceptions.

When too many recursive relationships occur, odds are strongly in favor that the data modelers are new and trying out all the neat stuff they learned in class or from some recently read book.

8

Preparing for Physical Database Design

"And when we see the figure of the house,
Then must we rate the cost of the erection,
Which if we find outweighs ability,
What do we then but draw anew the model
In fewer offices, or at least desist
To build at all?"   SHAKESPEARE

"The computer is a moron."   PETER DRUCKER

If you are both the logical data modeler and the physical database designer, then you know what information you need to build a database. But in many organizations the logical data modeler and physical database designer are two different people, possibly located in two separate and geographically dispersed organizations. In this situation, the logical data modeler has the more difficult task of anticipating what the physical database designer will need.

This chapter examines some of the information the logical data modeling process must produce so that it can be used as input to the physical database design process.

The Physical Database Design Process

Physical database design consists of building a database schema from the process and logical data models for a specified-systems environment. Whereas logical data models are very use-independent, the database design is quite use-specific.

The database design process is similar to assembling a puzzle. All the pieces are laid out at the beginning of the activity. The pieces are

TABLE 8.1   Database Design Steps

Step 1   Assume the Logical Data Model *is* the Physical Database Design

- Entities become record types
- Attributes become fields
- Relationships become database linkages

Step 2   Apply the processes documented in the process model against the database design

Step 3   Modify the database design to accommodate the systems environment and to improve database performance

Step 4   Repeat steps 2 through 3 as necessary

picked up, one at a time, and examined, and their fit into the overall picture assessed. Occasionally, a piece will be moved from its location as new and better fitting pieces are studied and added to the puzzle. In effect, physical database design is the iterative process of analyzing functions and applying those identified in the process model to the data model (Table 8.1).

The best way to understand the database design process is by example. Figure 8.1 is a data model for a stock brokerage securities processing system. The volumes that need to be handled by the system are as follows:

Entity	Occurrences
Customer	30,000
Account	50,000
Account Activity	500,000
Security	3,000

Start by applying the four Database Design Steps to the model. Make the logical data model a database design (step 1). The entities are now record types, attributes are fields, and relationships are linkages. (You can either create a separate diagram or use the logical data model diagram.)

Then, apply the processes to the database design (step 2). To make things simple, let's assume that the application has only one process:

Process: Fetch Security Activity

Volume: 3000 transactions per day
   On-line 0
   Batch 3000
Priority: Low

The process can now be applied to the data model, but first it must be converted to a Data Service Request (DSR). For example:

Fetch Security Activity: DSR

- Fetch all Activity occurrences where ACTIVITY DATE equals current date
- Within Account
- Within Security

The DSR can then be mapped against the database design, producing a Data Service Access Map (DSAM) (Fig. 8.2).

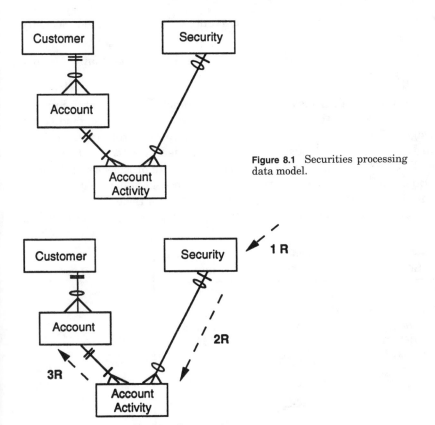

Figure 8.1 Securities processing data model.

Figure 8.2 Securities processing data service access map.
Transaction: Fetch security activity.

The arrows indicate how the record types would be accessed:

- From outside (initial database call) or
- From another record type

and the number indicates the sequence or order of access (1, 2, 3,...), while the letter indicates the type of database call:

- R   Read
- W   Write
- D   Delete
- U   Update

The map should be read as follows:

1. Enter the database at the Security record type and read the first Security occurrence.

2. Read the Account Activity occurrences for the selected Security occurrence.

3. Read the Account occurrences for the selected Account Activity occurrences.

The output for this transaction might look something like that in Fig. 8.3.

Now move on to the third step. To maximize performance, modify the design of the database to reflect the systems environment, i.e., the hardware that will house the database, system software (including the DBMS that will be used), and location of the processors and data.

Based on the Fetch Security Activity process, you might conclude that the Activity occurrences should be stored on the same database page as the Security occurrence to which it is related. The physical

Security	Activity		Account
Siddall Ltd	Buy	100 Shares	12345
Rowley Inc	Buy	200 Shares	25466
Chatterton Inc	Sell	140 Shares	43435
Rossetti Corp	Buy	1,000 Shares	12345

Figure 8.3 Report output.

database designer will want to include in the design the techniques and features of the DBMS to be used. In our example, this is hashing and clustering.

- Hashing is a technique for storing a record on a database page based on the value of its key. (If you know the page a record is stored on, you can directly access the record, avoiding the need to read costly indices.) For example, assume the key of the Employee occurrence is '12345678,' and 1000 pages are in the database. The simplest hashing scheme is to divide the key by the number of pages (12345678/1000 = 12,345 with a remainder of 678). Add 1 to the remainder (679), and this is the page the DBMS should use to store the occurrence.

- Clustering is a technique for storing a record on the same page as another record occurrence—often the record that is normally accessed just prior to the target record. In the above example, you might want to store the Account Activity occurrences on the same database page as its related Security occurrence to reduce physical I/O.

At this point, it is appropriate to replace the logical modeling graphic symbols with symbols closer to those used for the physical database management system, e.g., replace boxes with record types and arrows with pointers or symbolic keys (Fig. 8.4).

Each database design should have a design rationale that explains every change made to the original design created in step 1. As a sort of journal of the changes made to the design (e.g., additional processes are added or the volumes change), it helps the database designer to more easily understand how new or future changes will affect the database design. It is particularly useful for documenting and reviewing a database design.

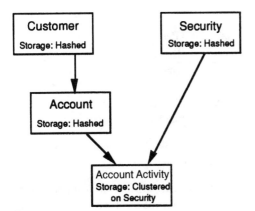

Figure 8.4 Securities processing database design.

Example: Database design rationale

- Security is hashed, since it is the entry into the database.
- Account is hashed, since:

  Currently there is no use for Customer (and if there continues to be no use for it, the record type will be dropped from the database).

  Account cannot be clustered around Account Activity. Account is at the "one" end of a "one-to-many" relationship. (Physical designers rarely cluster a record type that sits at the "one" end of a relationship around the record type at the "many" end.)

- Account Activity will be clustered around Security because it improves performance.

The last point in the design rationale—the performance consideration—is the most important. In most applications the most expensive function is physical I/O. CPU cycles and communications lines are expensive to be sure, but for most applications, the approach that can reduce physical I/Os is usually the cheapest and fastest. So performance efforts should focus on trying to reduce physical I/Os.

In the example above, the ratio between Security and Account Activity is 1:167, and the ratio between Account and Account Activity is 1:10. This means that for each Security occurrence read, the DBMS will have to perform 167 logical I/Os for Account Activity and 17 additional logical I/Os for Account, for a total of 184 logical I/Os per Security record read.

But there are cheaper and faster alternatives. If Account, Account Activity and Security are all hashed, then the transaction will need 184 physical I/Os. However, if Account Activity is clustered around Account, then the number of physical I/Os drops to 168. But the best approach of all is clustering Account Activity around Security, which lowers the physical I/Os to 18. Based on this analysis, the best database design would cluster Account Activity around Security.

	Physical I/Os Per	
Account Activity	DSR	Night
Hashed	184	552,000
Clustered on Account	168	504,000
Clustered on Security	18	54,000

How Logical Data Modeling and Physical Database Design Differ

As noted earlier, logical data modeling is quite different from physical database design. Whereas logical design is concerned with abstracting and constructing a representation of an organization, physical design is concerned with transforming the various analysis models into a physical reality. The logical data modeler must be adept at interviewing staff, drawing out important information and conceptualizing the meaning of the raw data. The physical database designer, on the other hand, must be able to

- Merge a number of logical models dealing with data, processes, and the systems environment.
- Resolve conflicts for resources from competing applications and/or users.
- Produce a workable physical design of the system that maximizes benefits at minimum cost (Table 8.2).

The physical designer must contend with a lot more that just the data models. Typically, at least three sources of information are examined by the physical database designer (Fig. 8.5):

- Data model
- Process model(s)
- Systems environment

    DBMS

    Hardware

    Network

    Location of the system components

The physical database designer must interpret all of these models and produce the appropriate database design. The most important skill the designer must exhibit is the ability to balance competing needs and correctly manage the tradeoffs. An example will help illustrate this point.

TABLE 8.2   Differences Between Data Modeling and Database Design Skills

Necessary Logical Data Modeling Skills	Necessary Database Design Skills
• Conceptualization (see world logically) • Abstraction • Interview skills • Good "people" skills • Ability to uncover facts	• Understanding of hardware and software usage • Concrete thinking • Work well with systems staff • Uncover and manage tradeoffs (balance competing needs)

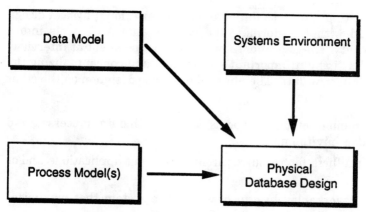

Figure 8.5 Physical database design process.

Rossetti Perpetual Care Cemetery is building an order processing system consisting of three record types:

- Customer
- Order
- Product

All accesses of Order are either through Customer or Product (i.e., all Orders relate to a specific Customer or Product). Further, the Customer and Product record occurrences are stored using a hashing technique so that a single occurrence of either can be accessed with one physical I/O. (For this exercise, hashing has been simplified. All hashed accesses are only one physical I/O; in reality, a more realistic number would be between 1.0 and about 1.3 physical I/Os per access). If Order is also stored using the hashing technique, then fetching one Customer record and one Order record will require two physical I/Os. Likewise, two I/Os are also required to fetch one Product and one Order record.

If, instead, the Order occurrence is stored on the same page as its related Product occurrence, then both the related Product and Order records can be fetched with a single physical I/O. However, the Customer and related Order occurrences will still require two I/Os.

On the other hand, if the appropriate Order occurrence is stored on the same page as the related Customer occurrence, then the Customer/Order fetch will take a single I/O. But now, fetching a Product/Order pair will require two physical I/Os.

Unfortunately, Order can be stored on the same page as the related Product occurrence, or on the same page as the related Customer occurrence, but not both. Which record, Product or Customer should Order be stored close to?

The answer is not immediately obvious. What is obvious is that the choice involves a tradeoff. You can either have the Customer/Order I/Os or the Product/Order I/Os, but not both.

The physical designer must find a method to weigh the advantages and disadvantages of each option and decide on the one that best serves the organization. In this case the physical designer will have to look to the process model(s) to resolve the situation. By examining the types of processes that use the data, their volumes and their priorities, the designer can usually come to a decision about which approach maximizes benefits and minimizes disadvantages. In Rossetti's case, the decision was to store the Order record on the Customer page since the number of times Order is fetched from the Customer occurrence far exceeded the Product/Order fetch.

Tradeoffs are probably the toughest part of physical database design and the part that requires the most input from the various logical models. The difficulty facing both logical and physical staff alike is identifying exactly what data the designer will need to perform the critical tradeoffs.

Let's re-examine the securities example used earlier. For purposes of this discussion, however, we will add complexity by creating another process.

Process: Fetch Customer Activity

Volume: 100,000 transactions per day
   On-line 65,000
   Batch 35,000
Priority: High

The Data Service Request might look like that in Table 8.3. Plotting this DSR on the model creates the Data Service Access Map in Fig. 8.6. The output for this transaction might look something like that in Fig. 8.7. This second process puts a different light on the database design. The Data Service Access Maps show that the two processes need to access Account and Account Activity data, but from opposite directions. If you limit your choices to just the question of which records should be hashed and which clustered, you are left with two possibilities.

TABLE 8.3   Example of a Data Service Request

> ## DSR: Fetch Customer Activity
>
> - Fetch all Activity occurrences
> - Within Account
> - Within Customer

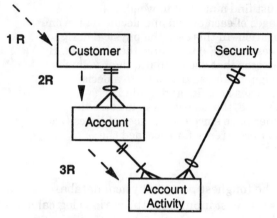

Figure 8.6 A data service access map. Transaction: Fetch customer activity.

Customer	Account	Activity	Security
Smith	12345	Buy 100 Shares	Siddall
Smith	25466	Buy 200 Shares	Rowley
Jones	43435	Sell 140 Shares	Chatterton
Jones	43435	Buy 1,000 Shares	Rossetti

Figure 8.7 Report output.

Option A: The logical I/Os for the new process are

- Customer   1.0
- Account   1.7
- Account Activity   <u>17.0</u>
- Total   19.7 L I/O

Because the Account Activity record is clustered around Security, the number of physical I/Os are

- Customer   1.0
- Account   1.7
- Account Activity   17.0
- Security   <u>0.0</u>
- Total   19.7 P I/O

Which gives a total number of daily physical I/Os of

- On-line   1,280,500
- Batch   <u>689,500</u>
- Total   1,970,000 P I/O

The second database option, Option B, is to cluster Account Activity around Account (Fig. 8.8). By running through the arithmetic, you can construct an argument as to the most acceptable option (Table 8.4). Option B appears to be the better choice for the database design, assuming Options A and B were the only options and competing requests for service.

What you have just completed is step 4, i.e., to repeat steps 2 through 3 as necessary.

This example, of course, is artificial. The tradeoff "Should Account Activity be stored clustered around Account or Security?" was designed to be purely mathematical. In many cases, the database designer must also consider on-line performance versus batch performance, differing priorities for the transactions, and the risk to the business from poor response time or not completing a report on time. Many of the decisions relating to competing requests for service will, in fact, be quite subjective, which makes the job of the designer rather difficult. In fact, if the designer is not cautious, the designer could potentially satisfy nobody in an attempt to serve everybody.

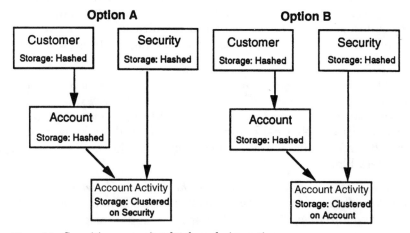

Figure 8.8 Securities processing database design options.

TABLE 8.4   Clustering Options

DSR	Option A Physical I/Os		Option B Physical I/Os	
Fetch Security Activity	Batch	54,000	Batch	504,000
	On-Line	0	On-Line	0
	Total	54,000	Total	504,000
Fetch Customer Activity	Batch	1,280,500	Batch	175,000
	On-Line	689,500	On-Line	94,500
	Total	1,970,000	Total	269,500
Grand Total	Batch	1,334,500	Batch	679,000
	On-Line	689,500	On-Line	94,500
	Total	2,024,000	Total	773,500

The Role of the Logical Data Modeler in Physical Database Design

As you no doubt have (or will) discover, the information necessary to make all important judgment calls is not always available to the physical database designer. Since incomplete methodologies, missing or incomplete analysis deliverables, and errors conceal important data, the logical data modeler should be aware of these problems and work to keep the physical designer informed.

Information that the logical data modeler should give to the physical database designer is of three types:

- *Formal deliverables defined by the system development methodology, techniques, and tools.* These deliverables are required outputs of the project and usually determined by the organization, product vendor, or project team before the project starts. Simply stated, they are what you have to do to say you are done.

- *Informal outputs, such as information which might be needed by the physical designer but is not included in the methodology, technique, or tool deliverables.* These are the things that the logical data modeler believes the physical database designer needs to know to correctly design the database. (Informal output will be discussed in more detail later in this chapter.)

- *Informal notes, suggestions, or tips the logical designer feels are important for the physical designer to be aware of to do the job efficiently and effectively.* This third category includes insights that the logical modeler wants to share with the physical designers. The subject can be logical or physical in nature. In fact, the subject can be anything that may support the physical designer in fulfilling the database mandate.

In the case of informal outputs and notes, the logical designer has the opportunity to communicate concerns, insights, and any information that does not fit into the formal deliverables, i.e., information that is needed but cannot, or should not, be bundled into a predetermined (formal) package. For example, an attribute VENDOR NUMBER may not be unique and, therefore, will not be specified as an identifier. Yet, this nonuniqueness might be in less than 1 percent of the cases. If so, this information should be passed on to the physical database designers.

Likewise, during logical data modeling the modeler should only be thinking about logical issues, but controlling thoughts is simply not possible. When a flash appears about how something should be done physically, the modeler should do three things:

- Write it down.

- However, ignore it when building the logical data model.

- And, at the end of logical data modeling, review the bits collected and pass the ones that still make sense on to the physical database designer *as comments*.

The following is a look at a number of areas where information over and above the deliverables is useful and perhaps needed by the physical designer.

Unique and almost unique identifiers

Logical data modeling identifies which attributes are identifiers and which are descriptors. Physical designers use the identifiers for primary and secondary (index) keys in the database schema. In most situations, primary keys are unique, but not in all cases. Secondary keys are sometimes unique, but rarely is their uniqueness a DBMS requirement.

There are certain logical data modeling attributes that are not 100 percent unique but are, in practice, rarely duplicated. For example, one university uses a four digit sequential code within year as a student number. The code works as follows: Take the last digit of the year the student is scheduled to graduate and make it the first digit of the student number. Thus, all student numbers for the class of 1996 will start with a '6.' The next four digits are sequentially assigned. The first student to matriculate in the class of 1996 is given the student number 60001. The one thousandth four hundred and ninety-second student in the class of 1995 would have the student number 51492.

The only way this number could be repeated is if the one thousandth four hundred and ninety-second student from the class of 1985 or 1975, etc., were to come back to school. Since this is quite unlikely, the occurrence uniqueness factor for this attribute is probably above 99.9 percent. Uniqueness factors of 90 percent or more are of interest to physical designers and should be communicated to them.

A second type of almost unique identifier is an attribute which is unique only during part of its life. For example, a business might be able to only guarantee that a number is unique for a certain period of time. This information should also be conveyed to the database designers.

Uniqueness algorithms

As stated earlier, not all entities will have identifiers. Identifiers will be assigned only to those entities that have "natural" business identifiers. Logical data modelers should not arbitrarily create artificial attributes to make an entity unique. Where no natural identifier exists, the physical database designer will have to create a unique key for the record type, if one is required. In these instances, a sequential number is often used.

However, even when logical data modelers are not comfortable specifying an identifier, they may have insight as to what a generated number should look like. For example, a combination of two or three "non-unique" fields might give 99 percent uniqueness. Or a descriptor code could be appended to an attribute. Take the example of the Social Security Number (SSN) in the US and the Social Insurance Number (SIN) in Canada. The analyst would know that an append "U" (for US) to the nine-digit SSN and "C" (for Canada) to the nine-digit SIN will result in a field that was unique across both countries.

Class membership actual counts and ratios

Most tools require that the analyst specify the number of entity occurrences. But as noted earlier in the securities processing database design example, database designers are also concerned with ratios between entities. In the security firm example, there were 3000 Security occurrences and 500,000 Account Activity occurrences—a ratio of 1:167. If Account Activity is clustered around Security, then each database page must be able to handle 168 occurrences. However, if there are 5,000,000 Account Activity occurrences, then the ratio is 1:1667, and each page must be able to accommodate 1668 occurrences—a feat most database management systems would find difficult to perform. If an occurrence cannot be on the desired page, then the system must figure out some other place to store it—all of which will consume resources and degrade performance. The database designer must be aware of these situations and take them into account.

The distribution of the occurrences can also affect the database design. Take again the example of the Security/Account Activity ratio of 1:167. Two databases could have the same ratio but perform quite differently based on the standard deviation of the ratio. Take the first database, in which 90 percent of the Security occurrences are linked to between 142 and 192 Account Activity occurrences (plus or minus 25 on either side of the average of 167), and the second database where only 40 percent fall within the same range. The second database is more likely to have "off page" records than the first, since the chance of exceeding the maximum number of records per page is greater in the second database than in the first.

Whenever possible the logical data modeler should convey to the physical database designer not only the number of occurrences of an entity and the cardinality and modality of its relationships but also information about the maximums, minimums, averages, and standard deviations which can affect database performance. Moreover, since entity ratios are very sensitive to changes caused by the entity growth rate, growth rate information should also be specified.

9

Object-Oriented Modeling

"For a list of all the ways technology has
failed to improve the quality of life, please
press three."   ALICE KAHN

"He was a bold man that first ate an oyster."
                                   SWIFT

In the past, significant improvements in software productivity proved to be elusive. Structured techniques, methodologies, fourth generation languages, relational database management systems, and CASE tools all were attempts to attack the system development log jam, significantly reduce costs, and improve the quality of software development, and all have more or less failed.

One of the more recent approaches has focused on the concept of reusable code. Simply stated, the concept places emphasis on writing software routines once and then sharing them with all the programmers in an organization. This too has failed.

But the combination of a number of approaches, such as methodology and CASE, with the decades-old concept of object-oriented development, is making a bit of headway toward reusable code—and the accompanying productivity benefits—a reality. In fact, sufficient headway has been made to convince developers that this "new" approach could be the dominant force in systems development for the next decade or two.

If successful, the object-oriented approach will drastically change how applications are developed. As opposed to less successful approaches, object-oriented development tries to cover the whole spectrum of system development. There are

- Object-oriented methodologies
- Object-oriented analysis

- Object-oriented design
- Object-oriented modeling
- Object-oriented programming
- Object-oriented database management systems

If object-oriented development takes off, it will have an impact on most areas of the system development life cycle, including logical data modeling. Yet oddly enough, the knowledgeable logical data modeler is actually better positioned to understand and implement object-oriented concepts than any other system development professional. This chapter presents a brief overview of object-oriented modeling (much of which will sound familiar to you) and shows how it fits into the scheme of logical data modeling.

Object-Oriented Concepts

Object-oriented modeling is the focal point of object-oriented development. In it one finds the concepts that expose the very nature of the use of objects. As a starting point, let's review some of the object-oriented terminology.

Organizations or systems are concerned with, save information about, and/or process self-contained "things" called *objects*. Customers, Employees, Classrooms, Books, and Invoices are all examples of objects. Objects usually consist of data describing the object and a set of operations, also called behavior or methods, to manipulate the descriptive data.

Objects which share attribute types and operations are grouped together into object classes (sometimes just called classes). An object instance is an occurrence of an object class. For example, if Employee is an object class, then "Thomas Chatterton" is an object instance of the class Employee.

Objects consist of attributes and operations. Attributes are properties of object classes. Examples of attributes would be NAME, INVOICE NUMBER, COLOR, and TITLE. An attribute value is a property of an object instance. An operation is a process that accesses, manipulates, modifies, deletes, or creates one or more attributes. An operation might be 'Add New Customer,' or 'Pay Invoice.'

Objects are linked to other objects through

- Association
- Inheritance

Association is the natural relationship between objects. If you are modeling a business, then these associations are business relationships. For example, customers buy products, so there is a natural association between the objects Customers and Products called "buy." Associations can have cardinality (one-to-one, one-to-many, and many-to-many) and modality (optional and mandatory), and can exist between one, two, three, or more objects (unary, binary, or n-ary).

An object can inherit properties from other objects. Picture classes as organized into hierarchies with the most general objects at the top and the more specific at the bottom. The more specific objects, the subclasses, inherit attributes and operations from their more generic parents, their superclasses. For example, the objects Wholesale Customer and Retail Customer might be "children" of the superclass Customer. They inherit from Customer all of its attributes and operations. In addition, the children can have their own unique operations and attributes, and can function as parents to other objects.

Objects have specific boundaries such that what goes on inside an object is not related to what might be going on outside the object. This is called *encapsulation*. For example, the object Customer contains the operation "Add New Customer" and knows exactly what to do when the operation is invoked, while the same operation might be meaningless if applied to the object Product. The attributes and operations of the object Customer are hidden from other objects. In essence, the object is a black box which performs a task when the proper message is passed. What the task is and how it is performed are not known by any other object.

Objects communicate with other objects by passing messages back and forth. For example, the object Purchase might pass to the object Customer a message to change a customer's credit status. Because of encapsulation, Purchase does not need to know how Customer changes a credit status. In other words, the operations and attributes Customer will use or modify as a result of receiving the message, "Change Customer Credit Status," will be transparent to Purchase.

This information can be displayed on an object model. On the object model, an object is represented by a bold-lined box (Fig. 9.1).

Association and inheritance links are represented by solid lines. It is a good practice to label the line so that the link can be easily identified and understood (Fig. 9.2).

Attributes are listed either in the object box, if there are only a few of them, or in a separate document (Fig. 9.3). If the attributes in the

Figure 9.1 Object diagramming convention: An object is represented by a bold-lined box.

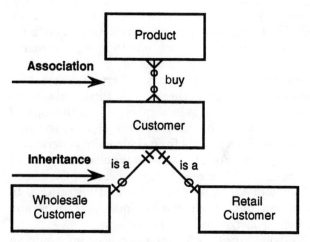

Figure 9.2   Association and inheritance diagramming conventions.

object can have a structure of their own, the object can have its own logical data model (Fig. 9.4).

Most object operations can be represented by a narrative describing the behavior. However, if the behavior is complex, any one of the numerous process modeling techniques, such as data flow diagramming, can be used (Fig. 9.5).

Messages are represented on the object model as dashed lines with an arrow showing the direction of the message movement (Fig. 9.6).

How Object-Oriented Analysis Works

As an example, let us look at the object-oriented analysis of the South Seas Company, a securities firm. The object model graphically represents the objects, structure, and interaction of the basic components of South Seas (Fig. 9.7).

If you remove the structure between the objects and just leave the messages, you have a process flow view of the object model (Fig. 9.8).

In like manner, if you remove the object messages, you are left with a diagram that resembles an Entity-Relationship diagram (ERD) (Fig. 9.9).

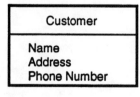

Figure 9.3 Attribute diagramming convention.

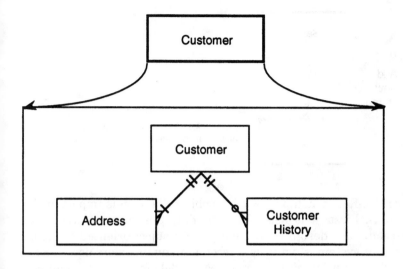

Figure 9.4 Logical data model for an object.

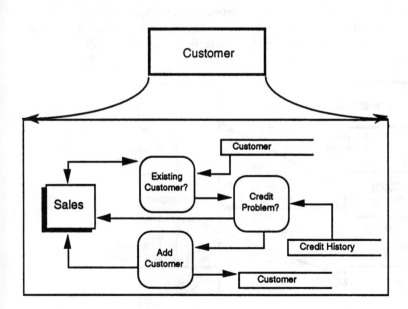

Figure 9.5 Data flow diagram for an object.

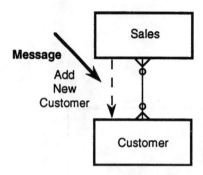

Figure 9.6 Message diagramming convention.

The Entity-Relationship view of the object diagram is important for two reasons. First, it is needed by the data designers to create the physical database design (particularly if an object-oriented database management system is not used). Second, many modelers use an ERD as a starting point for creating an object model since the tasks for creating an object model are similar to those for creating an Entity-Relationship model.

The object model

To create an object model, first identify the basic objects that are associated with the subject. The result is a list that looks like an entity list. Second, identify the associations between the objects. Third, diagram the objects using any of a number of emerging object-modeling conventions. The diagrams in this chapter are based on Entity-Relationship

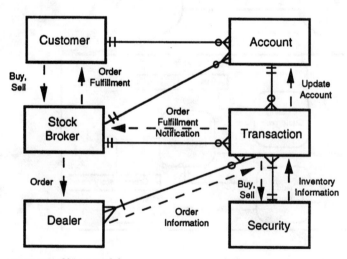

Figure 9.7   Object model.

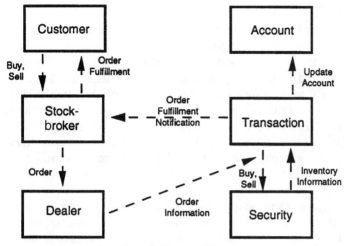

Figure 9.8   Process flow view of object model.

symbols, but others could be used. Fourth, the messages between the objects are added to the diagram.

When the object model is complete, attention should turn to what is going on inside each object. Both the object's attributes and operations need to be documented.

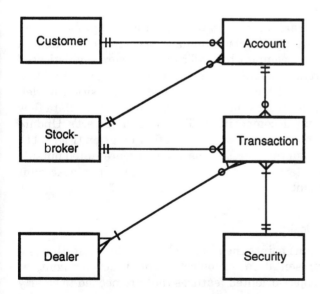

Figure 9.9   Entity-relationship view of object model.

Object model data

Documenting the data within an object is relatively simple since the attributes found in an object are either properties of that object or are properties of another object passed in a message. For example, as part of a message, the Transaction object could pass the attribute TRANS-ACTION NUMBER to the Stock Broker object. TRANSACTION NUMBER is a property of Transaction and not Stock Broker, even though the operations of both objects use the attribute. TRANSACTION NUMBER is defined in the Transaction object, so it does not need to be redefined in the Stock Broker object. Data only needs to be documented once, so data belonging to other objects only needs to be documented in the owner object.

In most cases, the data in an object has no structure. By structure we mean that if the data were on an ERD, it would be in multiple entities—an object with no data structure means that all of its attributes would be in a single entity on an ERD.

When there is no data structure, documenting an object's data is limited to specifying its definition and domain. If, however, an object's data has structure, then the structure should be modeled in an object ERD fragment. For example, if the data for the Account object includes static account information as well as numerous activity items, then the analyst would represent the one-to-many relationship between Account and Account Activity in a mini-ERD (Fig. 9.10).

Object model operations

If the object operations are uncomplicated, then they are probably best documented using a simple English language narrative or structured English technique. More complex behavior needs a more sophisticated documentation approach. Event-oriented processes might require a dynamic process modeling technique such as state transition modeling, while more static processes could use techniques such as data flow modeling or functional decomposition. The Account object's Update Account operation is documented with a data flow diagram (Fig. 9.11). Note how in the diagram the object Transaction is represented outside the object box as an external entity, and the message Update Account is a data flow to Account.

The obscure object of desire

There are two important points the reader should note. First, this is a very simplified representation of object-oriented development; it ignores many other object-oriented features that are needed to clearly

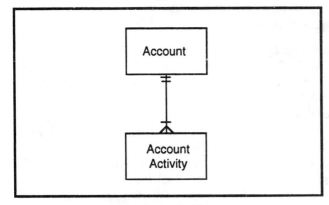

Figure 9.10   Object entity relationship fragment.

understand object-oriented development. Unfortunately, adequately exploring them is beyond the scope of this book.

The second point is that object-oriented modeling is in its infancy. How objects are represented and how the symbols should be used are in the early stages of evolution. Current approaches vary widely, and no matter how much developers might desire some standardization, this situation is likely to continue, if not accelerate, for at least the near term. Nonetheless, this example does represent the basic object-oriented modeling concepts—at least one approach.

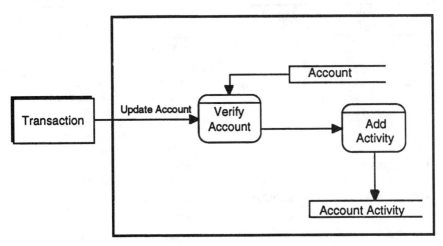

Figure 9.11   Object data flow diagram.

The Relationship between Object-Oriented Modeling and Logical Data Modeling

Object-oriented modeling and logical data modeling have much in common. The concepts of the former, in fact, are quite similar to those of the latter (as shown below). But, despite the many similarities, a number of differences also exist. The uniqueness of object-oriented modeling is the marrying of data and process into the same basic entities (Table 9.1).

What should be obvious is that the well-prepared logical data modeler will have much less difficulty digesting the concepts of object-oriented modeling than the average process modeler. So much of the object-oriented approach is similar to the logical data modeling approach that one could consider object-oriented modeling an extension of logical data modeling—and to a certain extent it is.

Another major similarity is that both approaches share the difficulty that many analysts have of merging the concepts of data and process in such a way that data is not subservient to process. This is the reason those who study, understand, and build applications based on object-oriented modeling tend to be those who also have a good understanding of logical data modeling concepts. Good approaches stick together.

The Advantages of Object-Oriented Modeling

As was mentioned in the beginning of this chapter, one advantage of object-oriented modeling is that it provides an environment in which

TABLE 9.1   Comparison of Object-Oriented Modeling and Logical Data Modeling

Object-Oriented Modeling	Logical Data Modeling	Differences
▪ Object	▪ Entity	▪ Object includes processes
▪ Attribute	▪ Attribute	▪ None
▪ Link	▪ Relationship	▪ Similar —Associations are the same —Inheritance the same as subtype/supertype except data modeling does not include operations
▪ Encapsulation		▪ No corresponding logical data modeling concept
▪ Object Class	▪ Entity Type	▪ None
▪ Object Instance	▪ Entity Instance	▪ None
▪ Messages		▪ No corresponding concept, since messages are process related

concepts such as reusable code can become a reality. It also solves another problem. As noted in Chap. 5, neither the data nor the process model can express all of an organization's rules. Some, but not all, rules are expressible in the process model and some, but not all, in the data model. Object-oriented modeling, however, does provide a single place where all business rules can be expressed.

Object-oriented modeling also brings together process and data modeling without making the technique of one subservient to the technique of the other. It does this by affirming that while both data and process are properties of an object, they each need a different approach to communicating their richness.

10

Some Final Thoughts

*"There is no expedient to which a man will
not go to avoid the labor of thinking."*
THOMAS EDISON

*"The universe is full of magical things
patiently waiting for our wits to grow
sharper."*   EDEN PHILLPOTTS

Data modeling is difficult. As we have seen in the previous chapters, good data modeling involves mastering well-defined concepts, such as terminology and conventions. It also requires considerable, and sometimes subjective, expertise in a strongly experience-based process.

Recognizing that many data modeling efforts are not successful, this book thus far has dealt with the most prevalent reason for failures, namely, insufficient knowledge of data modeling concepts. While there are no guarantees in life except death and taxes (if Benjamin Franklin is to be believed), you can feel confident that by following the guidelines and rules of thumb described in this book, your system development expertise should improve.

The tutorials in Chaps. 3, 4, and 5, as well as the principles, guidelines, and rules of thumb, offer a solid foundation for the analyst who is looking to data model correctly. What has not been discussed yet are two other causes for failure, namely:

- The belief that technology can substitute for skill

- Not enough resources or time invested—in the classroom and on the job—in developing necessary skills

We will now rectify that situation.

Tools: Aids or Inhibitors?

The results of installing new tools are predictable to those who have already been through it. But like the hot stove and the child, the cautions of the experienced are often ignored until the pain is felt firsthand. Nevertheless, let's examine in more detail the problems many organizations have with tools (using CASE as the focal point)—and recognize that the same issues apply equally to the use of methodologies and techniques.

The purposes of development aids and tools are to remove impediments, simplify or automate mindless or near-mindless tasks, and make it easier for humans to do what they do best—think the problem through. Although CASE tools have the potential to change how people design applications, two perceptions inhibit their success, namely, that these tools

- Are easily understood and usable
- Can replace or substitute for human thought

Adhering to either one can hinder productivity gains and potentially jeopardize the success of the project.

Most of the time-related disappointments expressed by companies can be attributed to a lack of CASE experience in general, and to learning curve problems in specific. The learning curve is the amount of time it takes an analyst to learn how to use the tool to complete a task without outside help (Fig. 10.1).

In reality, it takes many projects and years before all the developers in an organization learn CASE. However, a simple learning curve explanation does not sufficiently describe the fundamental problem. An example can best express this.

Think back to your days in school. If your school days were more than just a few years ago, you probably had to type term papers on a typewriter rather than on a word processor, as so many students do

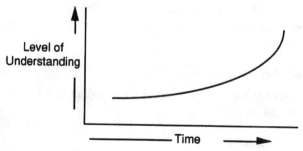

Figure 10.1 A classic learning curve.

today. How did you do it? If you were like most students, you sat down with your reference materials, a pad, and a pen, and wrote the paper out in long hand. After numerous revisions it was time for the type-writer—usually about 3:00 A.M. on the day the paper was due. By class time the paper was typed and, short of some erasures, ready to be handed in.

By contrast, newspaper reporters have traditionally typed stories on a manual typewriter without a hand-written draft. Most people cannot do this—they can write, or they can type, but not do both at the same time. (If they do both, the result is usually atrocious writing, bad typing, or both.) If you ask reporters how they do it, they will tell you that the feat is accomplished with a lot of practice.

The same can be said about driving a car. In the beginning, when you learn to drive, every action, such as shifting gears, requires a lot of thought—so much thought that you're sometimes unaware of what is happening on the road. It generally takes a long time before you "know" how to drive. With sufficient practice, the task becomes easy.

Now let's look at CASE installations. The hardware and software are installed, the training class fresh in the minds of the analysts, and the next day the analyst sits at a CASE tool designing a new system. See a problem? Developers are expecting too much too soon. People are simply not able to build a system with so little CASE experience. Knowledgeable sources indicate that the learning curve for these tools is from 30 days to 3 months.

But there is another curve that is even more important and, time-wise, further out than the learning curve. It is the internalization curve, which can be an order of magnitude or more beyond the learning curve (Fig. 10.2). Remember the automobile example? The new driver might learn to drive in a few days, but it takes much longer before the process is sufficiently internalized so that car handling becomes automatic. The driver eventually discovers that even while engrossed in conversation or thought, the body makes the right moves, such as stopping the car when needed and applying gas at the right time. Some drivers say that they can daydream and suddenly find themselves home after having successfully, and presumably lawfully, navigated many miles.

The same lesson applies to data processing as well. Take COBOL programmers and send them to a C programming language class. Within a few days they can correctly program in C, but more than likely, they will still be thinking in COBOL. The transition to thinking in C and purging the COBOL way of doing things can easily take 6 months or more of full-time C programming.

In like manner, the analyst or designer will know how to push a mouse around the CASE tool long before thinking in CASE can occur.

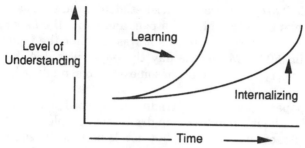

Figure 10.2   Learning vs. internalizing.

Learning this new environment will take at least as long as it took the programmer to think in the C language.

What does this mean for organizations? Simply that when introducing totally new concepts such as techniques, methodologies, or tools, organizations need to be more realistic about their expectations and the effectiveness of these concepts in the hands of inexperienced staff.

The Quality of Tool-Based Applications

A second problem many organizations have experienced is an unexpected deterioration of quality with tool-based systems, caused primarily by insufficient or incomplete analysis. Apparently, the level of thinking goes down as the tools are introduced.

Why does this occur? To a certain extent, this quality problem has always existed. Systems developers are much better at collecting and documenting data than they are at interpreting what data means. This is unfortunate, since the major contribution an analyst can bring to system development is the thought process itself (Fig. 10.3).

Some of the blame can be placed on the shoulders of the CASE vendors. Brochures and video tapes need action-oriented material. From a selling perspective, thinking is boring while mousing is action, excitement, and adventure. Moreover, thinking is hard work, and how better to sell a tool than to say it reduces hard work.

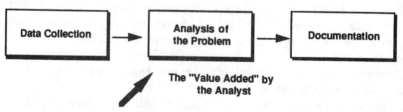

Figure 10.3   The analysis task. Many developers shortchange the analysis task.

The internalization curve also plays a significant role. Analysts and designers simply cannot handle the tool and think at the same time—at least not for some considerable period of time.

One Company's Solution

The picture painted above is not very pretty. In fact, many organizations have voiced disappointment with their tool-use efforts, citing that the promised productivity improvements have not materialized. A few have even reported negative results. For instance, in some situations tool-based applications are taking longer and/or costing more to develop than applications built without tools.

As good as CASE tools are, many organizations will continue to be disappointed with them, even though the fault really lies with the approach to managing the changes that the tools represent. How do you get around this problem? By following the rules you probably followed while you were typing all those college term papers—think first, "tech" later.

New techniques, methodologies, and tools represent significant change that must be introduced with skill and understanding. Most of all, the tools have to be introduced in a way so that they do not disrupt the most important ingredient to building a system—and the only one, at least for the time being, that cannot be automated—thinking.

That's not news to successful system builders. The successful construction of the most sophisticated and accurate systems resulted from careful and exact thought, not from the use of tools, techniques, or methodologies.

What steps can be taken to minimize the impact of problems when introducing CASE into an organization? The following approach was successfully pursued by one company:

- First, they did not purchase a CASE workstation for every developer. (This will also keep the accountants happy.)

- Second, they did require that all models—from process and data to action diagrams—be documented on paper before they were entered into the tool. This, in fact, was the underlying "secret" rationale for not providing a machine for each developer. The company indicated that they could not afford a machine for everybody, and thus machines would have to be shared. Sharing meant that the analysts and designers had to prepare their work before they sat down at the machine.

- Third, to reduce wasted time at the machine, all team members were asked to walk through their output with at least one other team member before mousing the work.

- Fourth, when the work was fairly stable and completed, then and only then were the developers allowed to enter the data into the tool.

What this organization did was to impose on the analysts and designers the same sequencing for introducing techniques, methodologies, and tools that was described in Chap. 3. First introduce techniques. When they are understood, then introduce methodologies. When the methodology is internalized, then introduce the tools.

This approach need not go on indefinitely. Like newspaper reporters, eventually the analysts and designers will be able to think in front of their workstations. But until that time, the successful project team will separate the two activities and require that one be performed before the other to ensure that both are accomplished.

Though the focus of this example was on CASE tools, the lessons apply equally well to all tools, techniques, and methodologies. Time will be needed to learn to use them properly and to sufficiently understand what they can do, and perhaps more importantly, what they cannot do. And even more time will be needed to make their use second nature.

In the final analysis, organizations and practitioners must recognize that neither the technique, nor the methodology, nor the tool represents the value added of the logical data modeling process. Rather, the real value added is the thought and insight that only the developer can provide.

A Logical Data Modeling Exercise

"Experience is by industry achieved."
SHAKESPEARE

"A bad workman never gets a good tool."
THOMAS FULLER

Data modeling is not a highly regimented science. There are few real rules and only a handful of firm conventions. And whereas there are a few common concepts, their representation in the numerous data modeling and CASE tools varies widely. The morass of different styles and conventions could make using different tools a headache.

A more serious problem occurs when the tool you are using does not accommodate the collection and storage of data you consider critical. For example, suppose the business requires that no more than 12 line item entity occurrences can be associates for any order entity occurrence. This is important information that many tools cannot accommodate. Where do you put it? Well, most tools have a comments field where the analyst can include important but unformatted information. The tool cannot act on this data, but it can usually be included in reports and on screens.

In this section we present a simple business case and show how a number of popular data modeling and CASE tools represent the information.

The Business Case

The South Seas Company is a stock brokerage firm specializing in commercial accounts. The following facts are known about South Seas Company data:

- Accounts can be owned by either a customer or a South Seas trader.
- Sales representatives can support many customers but a customer has only one sales representative at a time.

- South Seas needs to keep a record of which sales representative supported which customers and when.
- Not all customers have accounts or sales representatives.
- Every trader has at least one account and may have many.
- A customer can have many accounts but need not have any.
- Customer history, such as former names or addresses, must be kept.
- It is important to know if customers are related to other customers.
- Accounts can be of two types: "Cash" and "Margin."
- Margin accounts must keep track of special credit data.
- Accounts have activity such as the account opening or closing and the buying and selling of securities.
- Each security is issued by one company, but a company can issue zero, one, or many securities.
- Issuing companies and margin accounts must have a credit status.
- A credit status can be for a company or a margin account but not both.

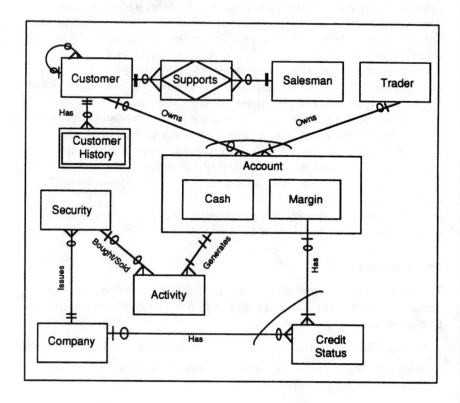

Entity Definition

Name: <u>Customer</u>   Entity Type <u>Proper</u>

Description: <u>An outside person, persons, or organization</u>
<u>we currently provide professional services to, or provided</u>
<u>services to in the past, or potentially will provide</u>
<u>services to</u> <u>in the near future.</u>

Synonyms: <u>Client</u>

Occurrences: <u>1.4 million</u>   Growth Rate: <u>7 percent annually</u>

Attributes	Type	Occurrences Type Percent
<u>Customer Name</u>	<u>Descrip</u>	<u>1:1</u> <u>100</u>
<u>Customer Address</u>	<u>Descrip</u>	<u>1:1</u> <u>100</u>
<u>Customer Type</u>	<u>Descrip</u>	<u>1:1</u> <u>100</u>
<u>Customer Number</u>	<u>Identif</u>	<u>1:1</u> <u>100</u>
<u>Foreign Resident Code</u>	<u>Descrip</u>	<u>0:1</u> <u>6</u>

Notes (IUD Rules, etc.): <u>Customer occurrences cannot be deleted</u>
<u>within one year of the last activity or if there is a</u>
<u>debit balance.</u>

Submitted by: <u>Thomas Rowley</u>   Date: <u>July 16, 1992</u>

Domain Definition

Name: Customer Number

Description: A six character integer between 100001 and
899999

Length Six characters

Format   6I

Abbreviations

Validation Rules

Default Values

Acceptable Values Integers between 100001 and 899999

Notes:

Submitted by: Thomas Rowley   Date: July 16, 1992

Relationship Definition

Name: Customer/Account_____Relationship Type: Binary_____

Description: A customer owns zero or more accounts._____
Ownership implies a legal ownership status._____

_____

_____

Entities:

Customer_____

Account_____

_____

Cardinality

    Maximum: Unlimited_____

    Minimum: Zero_____

    Average: 1.2_____

Modality Customer to Account optional, Account to Customer_____

mandatory_____

Notes: _____

_____

_____

_____

Submitted by: Thomas Rowley_____ Date: July 16, 1992_____

Attribute Definition

Name: Customer Number

Attribute Type: _____ Identifier

List Process (Action Diagram) Name if Attribute Type is "Derived"_____

Description: A six digit integer assigned sequentially

by the Credit Dept. to uniquely identify a customer

_____

_____

_____

_____

_____

Synonyms: Customer ID, Client ID and Client Number

Domain: Customer Number

Size: 6I

Notes: _____

_____

_____

_____

_____

Submitted by: Thomas Rowley   Date: July 16, 1992

Data Modeling and CASE Products

The following pages show how a number of data modeling and CASE tools would represent the preceding business case. Each of the tools is different, but they essentially share the same concepts even though they might express them differently. Only the product's data modeling characteristics are included. All of the tools, or in some cases the family of tools, provide some means of process modeling, and many will generate physical database design information. Nonlogical data modeling information has been intentionally left out.

The following data gives the modeler a taste of the different tools available. Some important notes. The data is representative and should not be considered complete. Only samples of the tool output are included. Lastly, the information presented is not intended to be an evaluation or critical review of the different products.

The business case was prepared by vendor staff, so if you have any questions about the product or its presentation, you should contact the vendor directly. Addresses, phone, and FAX numbers are provided.

Chen & Associates, Inc.
4884 Constitution Avenue
Suite 1-E
Baton Rouge, LA 70808
Phone (504) 928-5765
FAX (504) 928-9371

Product: ER-Modeler

Version 2.11 (DOS) and 3.01 (Windows)

The DOS version requires a PC with 640 kilobytes (KB) of low random-access memory (RAM) and a graphics card. For the Windows version, a 386 processor with 2-MB extended RAM and VGA graphics is recommended. For operating systems, version 3.1 or higher is needed for DOS and 3.0 or higher for Windows.

ER-Modeler is a family of products consisting of data modeling, process modeling, normalizing, reverse engineering, and schema generation tools. More than 30 DBMSs are supported. ER-Modeler links to most data dictionaries and CASE tools.

The logical data modeling tool, ER-Designer, supports many-to-many, n-ary, recursive, associative (called gerunds), and attributive relationships. Keys are not required.

As you would expect, ER-Modeler by Chen & Associates, Inc., will seem very familiar to you. The tool follows closely the approach to data modeling taken in this book.

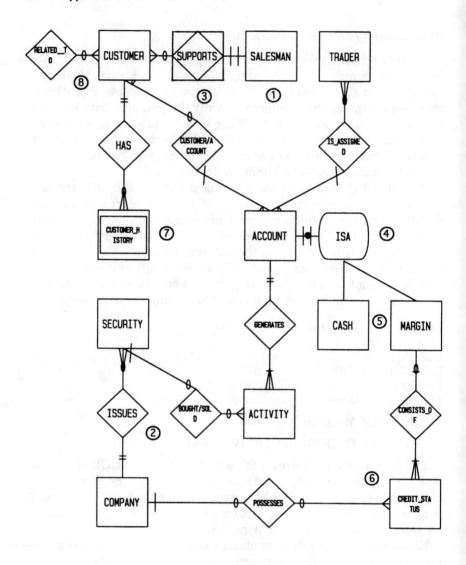

Southsea Diagram Report

DIAGRAM REPORT FOR 'SOUTHSEA'

Object Name : CUSTOMER   ENTITY
Alias   : CLIENT

Attributes List:

Name	Format	Key	Null
1: CUSTOMER_NUMBER	ID - N,6	Y	N

SC: FORMAT - A 6 DIGIT INTEGER BETWEEN 100001 AND 899999
LONG COMMENT:
An outside person, persons or organization we currently provide professional
services to, provided services in the past, or will provide services to in the near
future.   It is defined as a six digit integer assigned sequentially
by the Credit Dept. for identification purposes.

Synonyms: Customer ID, Client ID and Client Number

Domain: Customer Number

2: CUSTOMER_ADDRESS	C,35	N	N

SC: FORMAT - STREET ADDRESS

3: CUSTOMER_TYPE	C,10	N	Y

SC: RANGE - BUSINESS, GOVERNMENT OR INDIVIDUAL

4: FOREIGN_RESIDENT_CODE	C,3	N	N

SC: FORMAT - ABBREVIATION OF CUSTOMER'S COUNTRY

5: CUSTOMER_NAME	C,25	N	N

SC: FORMAT - LAST NAME, FIRST NAME OF CUSTOMER
LONG COMMENT:
Customer is an outside person, persons or organization we currently provide
professional services to, or provided services in the past, or potentially will
provide services to in the near future.

Synonyms: client

Occurrences: 1.4 million   Growth Rate: 7% annually

Rules: Customer occurrences cannot be deleted within one year of the last
activity or if there is a debit balance.

6: CITY	C,25	N	N

SC: FORMAT - CITY

7: STATE	C,2	N	N

SC: FORMAT - ABBREVIATION OF STATE

8: ZIP_CODE	N,5	N	N

SC: FORMAT - 99999

9: ACCOUNT_NUMBER	C,8	N	Y

SC: FORMAT - UNIQUE 8 CHARACTER STRING

LONG COMMENT:
A unique 8 character string assigned a customer who has an account.
Not all customers have salespersons or accounts.

10: SALESPERSON_ID	N,5	N	Y

SC: FORMAT - 99999

11: CUST_RELATIVES	C,72	N	Y

SC: FORMAT - 999999, 999999, ETC.
LONG COMMENT:
It is important to know which customers are related. The field is a list of the
format 999999, 999999, etc. Each number represents the corresponding
CUSTOMER_NUMBER of the relative(s) of a customer who are also customers.

From ENTITY   CUSTOMER
    To WEAK ENTITY CUSTOMER_HISTORY
Through RELATIONSHIP HAS

CARDINALITY	CARDINALITY
lower = 1	lower = 0
upper = 1	upper = N
lower n =	lower n =
upper n =	upper n =
average n =	average n =

Object Name : CUSTOMER_HISTORY   WEAK ENTITY
Alias   : HISTORY

Attributes List:

Name	Format	Key	Null
1: CUSTOMER_NUMBER		ID - N,6	Y

SC: formay - 999999

2: OLD_NAME	C,25	N	

SC: FORMER_NAME OF CUSTOMER

3: OLD_ADDRESS	C,35	N	

SC: FORMAT - STREET ADDRESS

4: OLD_CITY	N,25	N	

SC: FORMAT - CITY NAME

5: OLD_STATE	C,2	N	

SC: FORMAT - STATE ABBREVIATION

6: OLD_ZIP	N,5	N	

SC: FORMAT - 99999

From WEAK ENTITY CUSTOMER_HISTORY
    To ENTITY   CUSTOMER
Through RELATIONSHIP HAS

CARDINALITY   CARDINALITY
lower = 0   lower = 1
upper = N   upper = 1
lower n =   lower n = upper n =
upper n = average n =   average n =

Object Name : BOUGHT/SOLD   RELATIONSHIP
Alias   : BOUGHT/S

From RELATIONSHIP BOUGHT/SOLD
   To ENTITY   SECURITY

   CARDINALITY
   lower = 0
   upper = 1
   lower n =
   upper n =
   average n =

From RELATIONSHIP BOUGHT/SOLD
   To ENTITY   ACTIVITY

   CARDINALITY
   lower = 0
   upper = N
   lower n =
   upper n =
   average n =

Object Name : RELATED__TO   RECURSIVE

From RECURSIVE   RELATED__TO
   To ENTITY   CUSTOMER

   CARDINALITY
   lower = 0
   upper = N
   lower n =
   upper n =
   average n =

Notes about ER-Modeler Output

1. Entities are represented by a rectangle.

2. The standard relationship symbol is a diamond; as an alternative, a hexagon can be used. Class membership is designated by the characters "0," "1," and "n," which represent zero, one, and many, respectively, although crow's-feet also can be used.

3. An associative entity is represented by the standard diamond within a rectangle.

4. A rectangle with rounded corners is used to show generalization. The supertype is connected to the rounded rectangle with a line bisected by a solid circle.

5. Subtypes are connected to the generalization box without membership class indicators.

6. Exclusion is not represented.

7. Attributive entities are represented with a double-lined box.

8. Recursion is represented by a single relationship diamond and line.

Computer Systems Advisers, Inc.
50 Tice Boulevard
Woodcliff Lake, NJ 07575
Phone (201) 391-6500
FAX (201) 391-2210

Product: SILVERRUN-ERX

Version 2.1.1

Both Macintosh and PC versions are available. The Macintosh version requires 4 MB of main memory, the Windows 3.x version 6 MB, and the OS/2 version 8 MB.

One of a family of products, the data modeler, ERX (Entity Relationship Expert), supports attributive and associative entities (though the associative entity is represented as a relationship with attributes) and N-ary relationships. The tool allows many-to-many relationships and does not require unique identifiers or foreign keys.

An expert system allows the model to reflect business rules. Answering questions posed by ERX, the analyst introduces business rules into the tool. The rules are used to create data constraints such as cardinality and modality.

A separate product, SILVERRUN-RDM, can read ERX data and build two additional models: the logical data model and the database schema. The logical data model is a non-DBMS specific relational data model. Prime and foreign keys are added and many-to-many relationships are resolved into two one-to-many relationships with the introduction of an intersection table. The logical data model is used to create a relational DBMS schema. SILVERRUN supports most relational DBMSs.

Other SILVERRUN products include logical and physical process modeling tools. All tools use a common data dictionary.

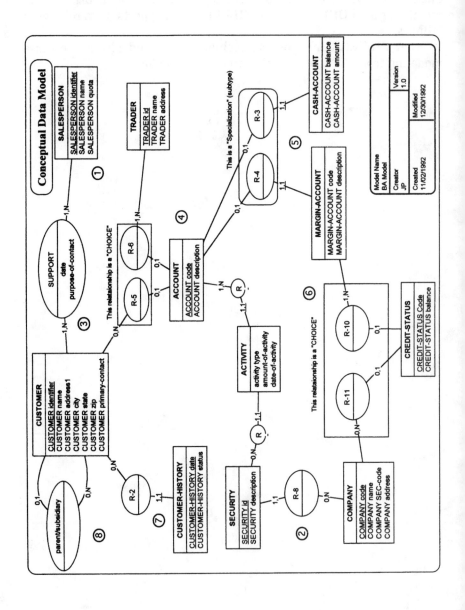

Conceptual Data Model

SALESPERSON
SALESPERSON identifier
SALESPERSON name
SALESPERSON quota
①

TRADER
TRADER id
TRADER name
TRADER address

CUSTOMER
CUSTOMER identifier
CUSTOMER name
CUSTOMER address1
CUSTOMER city
CUSTOMER state
CUSTOMER zip
CUSTOMER primary-contact

SUPPORT
date
purpose-of-contact
③

This relationship is a "CHOICE"

R-5   R-6

ACCOUNT
ACCOUNT code
ACCOUNT description
④

This is a "Specialization" (subtype)

R-4   R-3
⑤

CASH-ACCOUNT
CASH-ACCOUNT balance
CASH-ACCOUNT amount

MARGIN-ACCOUNT
MARGIN-ACCOUNT code
MARGIN-ACCOUNT description
⑥

ACTIVITY
activity type
amount-of-activity
date-of-activity

This relationship is a "CHOICE"

R-10   R-11

CREDIT-STATUS
CREDIT-STATUS Code
CREDIT-STATUS balance

COMPANY
COMPANY code
COMPANY name
COMPANY SEC-code
COMPANY address

SECURITY
SECURITY id
SECURITY description
R-8
②

CUSTOMER-HISTORY
CUSTOMER-HISTORY date
CUSTOMER-HISTORY status
R-2
⑦

parent/subsidiary
R-1
⑧

Model Name	
BA Model	
Creator	Version
JP	1.0
Created	Modified
11/02/1992	12/30/1992

200

Name	Ent. or rel.	P.	<1>	<2>	Domain	Len.	Dec.	Comment
ACCOUNT code	ACCOUNT	Y	N	N	CODE	4		
ACCOUNT description	ACCOUNT	N	N	N	DESC	40		
activity type	ACTIVITY	N	N	N	CODE	4		
amount-of-activity	ACTIVITY	N	N	N	AMOUNT	7	2	
date-of-activity	ACTIVITY	N	N	N	DATE			
CASH-ACCOUNT amount	CASH-ACCOUNT	N	N	N	AMOUNT	7	2	
CASH-ACCOUNT balance	CASH-ACCOUNT	N	N	N	AMOUNT	7	2	
COMPANY address	COMPANY	N	N	N	ADDRESS	35		
COMPANY code	COMPANY	Y	N	N	CODE	4		
COMPANY name	COMPANY	N	N	N	NAME	32		This is the official name of the company. Do not put the employee's nam...
COMPANY SEC-code	COMPANY	N	N	N	CODE	4		
CREDIT-STATUS balance	CREDIT-STATUS	N	N	N	AMOUNT	7	2	
CREDIT-STATUS Code	CREDIT-STATUS	Y	N	N	CODE	4		
CUSTOMER address1	CUSTOMER	N	N	N	ADDRESS	35		
CUSTOMER city	CUSTOMER	N	N	N	NAME	32		
CUSTOMER identifier	CUSTOMER	Y	N	N	ID	5		This identifier is a sequential number generated by the system by default.
CUSTOMER name	CUSTOMER	N	Y	N	NAME	32		
CUSTOMER primary-contact	CUSTOMER	N	Y	N	NAME	32		The primary contact is the person having signing authority.
CUSTOMER state	CUSTOMER	N	N	N	STATE	10		
CUSTOMER zip	CUSTOMER	N	N	N	ZIP	10		
CUSTOMER-HISTORY date	CUSTOMER-HISTORY	N	N	N	DATE			
CUSTOMER-HISTORY status	CUSTOMER-HISTORY	N	N	N	CODE	4		
MARGIN-ACCOUNT code	MARGIN-ACCOUNT	N	N	N	CODE	4		
MARGIN-ACCOUNT description	MARGIN-ACCOUNT	N	N	N	DESC	40		
SALESPERSON identifier	SALESPERSON	N	N	N	CODE	4		
SALESPERSON name	SALESPERSON	N	N	N	NAME	32		
SALESPERSON quota	SALESPERSON	N	N	N	AMOUNT	7	2	
SECURITY description	SECURITY	N	N	N	DESC	40		
SECURITY id	SECURITY	N	N	N	CODE	4		
date	SUPPORT	N	N	N	DATE			
purpose-of-contact	SUPPORT	N	N	N	DESC	40		
TRADER address	TRADER	N	N	N	ADDRESS	35		
TRADER id	TRADER	N	N	N	CODE	4		
TRADER name	TRADER	N	N	N	NAME	32		

12/18/1992

201

Name	Attributes	Comment
ACCOUNT	ACCOUNT code ACCOUNT description	This entity keeps track of all existing active accounts. Inactive accounts are NOT stored in this entity.
CASH-ACCOUNT	CASH-ACCOUNT balance CASH-ACCOUNT amount	
COMPANY	COMPANY code COMPANY name COMPANY SEC-code COMPANY address	
CREDIT-STATUS	CREDIT-STATUS Code CREDIT-STATUS balance	
CUSTOMER	CUSTOMER identifier CUSTOMER primary-contact CUSTOMER name CUSTOMER address1 CUSTOMER city CUSTOMER state CUSTOMER zip	This entity describes the customer as viewed by the organization.
CUSTOMER-HISTORY	CUSTOMER-HISTORY date CUSTOMER-HISTORY status	
MARGIN-ACCOUNT	MARGIN-ACCOUNT code MARGIN-ACCOUNT description	
SALESPERSON	SALESPERSON identifier SALESPERSON name SALESPERSON quota	
SECURITY	SECURITY id SECURITY description	
TRADER	TRADER id TRADER name TRADER address	

Notes about SILVERRUN-ERX Output

1. An entity is represented by the standard rectangle, but the attributes can be (although they need not be) displayed in the entity box.

2. Relationships are expressed using an oval with solid lines connecting the related entities. Membership class is designated by the characters "0," "1," and "n," representing zero, one, and many, respectively, on the relationship line.

3. There is no specific graphic for an associative entity. An associative entity is simply a relationship that has attributes.

4. Generalizations are represented by placing the "relationship" lines linking the supertype with the subtypes in a box with rounded corners.

5. Subtypes are differentiated from the supertype by the relationship lines—subtypes have only one, supertypes many.

6. Exclusion is shown by boxing the two "options" in a rectangle with squared corners.

7. Attributive entities are identified by underlining the membership class information for the relationship.

8. Recursion is represented by adding a unary relationship to the entity.

Intersolv, Inc.
3200 Tower Oaks Boulevard
Rockville, MD 20852
Phone: (301) 230-3200

Product: Excelerator II

Version 1.1

A PC-based product, both Windows and OS/2 (release 2.0 or greater) versions are available. A 486 is recommended with 16-MB main memory and a VGA monitor.

Excelerator produces a rather clean data model graphic. Associative, attributive, and generalization are supported, but there are few differentiating graphic symbols. Also supported are recursive, n-ary, and many-to-many relationships.

All entities must have a primary identifier. Foreign keys are optional. There are no specific graphic symbols for attributive and associative entities, although they are identified in the repository. However, a site can customize Excelerator symbols so that unique graphics can be created for associatives and attributives.

Excelerator is a full CASE product supporting process and data modeling as well as schema generation for DB2, SQL Server, IBM Database Manager, and many other SQL relational database management systems.

Repository data is output using the Q&E query language packaged with the tool.

Since the formation of Intersolv, created by the merger of Sage (a strong player in the application code generation market) with Index Technology (the creator of Excelerator), the marketplace is poised for some very strong process related links between upper and lower CASE worlds. We will have to see if the same is forthcoming on the data side.

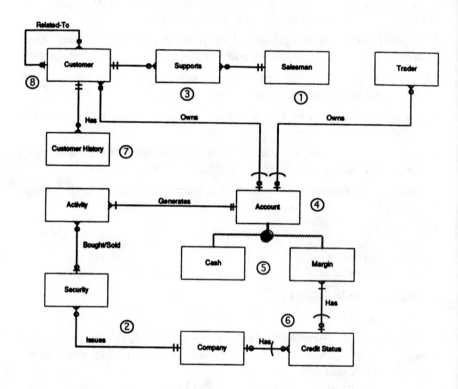

Entity Definition

Name	Synonyms	Description	Occurences	Growth Rate	Per	Purpose	Identifier	Attribute
Customer	Client	Memo	1400000	7	Y	F	Customer Number	Foreign Resident Code

An outside person, persons, or organization we currently provide professional services to, or provided services in the past, or potentially will provide services in the near future.

Customer Type
Customer Address
Customer Name

Relationship Definition

Name	Description	(1st) Entity	(1st) Min.	(1st) Med.	(1st) Max.	(2nd) Entity	(2nd) Min.	(2nd) Med.	(2nd) Max.
Customer-Account	Memo	Account	0	1,2	⑨ Many	Customer	1	1	1

A customer owns zero or more accounts. Ownership implies a legal status

Attribute Definition

Name	Description	Synonyms	Domain	Length	Storage Type
Customer Number	Memo	Customer ID, Client ID and Client Number	Customer Number	6	CH

A six digit integer assigned sequentially by the Credit Dept, to uniquely identify a cutomer

Domain Definition

Name	Description	Minimum Value	Maximum Value	Storage Type	Length
Customer Number	Memo	100001	899999	CH	6

A six character integer between 100001 and 899999

Notes about Excelerator Output

1. Entities are represented by the standard rectangular box.

2. Relationships are shown with a line. Labels are recommended but not mandatory. Membership class is represented by the crow's-feet notation.

3. Associative entities have no distinctive graphic. They appear as fundamental entities on the diagram but are listed as associatives in the repository.

4. Generalization is supported and depicted on the diagram with a black "ball" called a subtype set. The entities are linked with colored lines. The supertype relationship is delineated with a dark green line.

5. Subtypes are shown with rectangular boxes connected to the subtype/supertype with a light green line.

6. Exclusion is represented by an arch crossing the relationship line. If an entity is in more than one exclusive relationship, the arcs are numbered.

7. Attributive entities are supported, but there is no distinctive symbol. The repository will list the entity as attributive.

8. Recursion is represented by a single unary relationship.

9. Besides the standard minimum (modality) and maximum (cardinality), membership class also includes a medium column. You can enter the average number of occurrences participating in the relationship into this column. Since it is a text field, nonnumeric data can be entered. In the example, the analyst indicated that the average number of Accounts per Customer is between one and two.

KnowledgeWare, Inc.
3340 Peachtree Road NE
Suite 1100
Atlanta, GA 30326
Phone: (404) 231-3510

Product: Application Development Workbench

Release 2.7

Requires IBM Model 70 or greater or 100 percent compatible, with 12 to 16 MB of main memory, up to 60 MB of hard disk, PS/2 video graphics (VGA) display or 8514 display monitor, PS/2 bus, and serial or Microsoft mouse running under OS/2 1.3 or higher.

OS/2 based Application Development Workbench (ADW) is a series of tools supporting all phases of system development from planning through coding. Techniques supported are data modeling, process modeling (data flow diagramming and functional decomposition), structure charts, and DB2 schema generation.

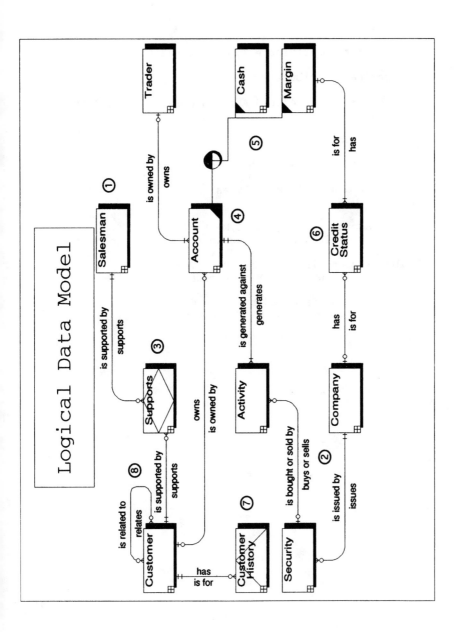

Logical Data Model

Entity Type: Cash

Attribute Types

*** No Attribute Types defined ***

Inherited Attribute Types

*** No Inherited Attribute Types defined ***

Relationship Types

*** No Relationship Types defined ***

Inherited Relationship Types

ID   Account.generates <1,M> Activity
        [is generated against   <1,1>   Account]

ID   Account.is owned by <0,1> Trader
        [owns   <1,M>   Account]

        Account.is owned by <0,1> Customer
        [owns   <0,M>   Account]

Entity Type Description Report - in Context: Subject Area Logical Data Model

Date   : 11-30-1992
Time   : 03:07:53 PM
Userid : BKR
Source : South Seas Corp.
         D:\ENC\SSC\

Entity Type: Account

    Attribute Types

        *** No Attribute Types defined ***

    Inherited Attribute Types

        *** No Inherited Attribute Types defined ***

    Relationship Types

    ID   generates <1,M> Activity
            [is generated against   <1,1>   Account]

    ID   is owned by <0,1> Trader
            [owns   <1,M>   Account]

          is owned by <0,1> Customer
            [owns   <0,M>   Account]

    Inherited Relationship Types

        *** No Inherited Relationship Types defined ***

- -

Information Type: Name

    PROPERTY   VALUE

    Created   1992/11/03 20:04:46 BKR
    Last Update   1992/11/03 20:04:46 BKR

    ASSOCIATION   TYPE   NAME

    Is Used by   Attribute Type   Customer.Name
                                                  Customer.Street 1
                                                  Customer.Street 2

```
Relationship Type: Company.has.Credit Status

    PROPERTY              VALUE

    Created               1992/11/03 19:51:18 BKR
    From To Maximum       M
    From To Minimum       0
    Last Update           1992/11/03 19:51:18 BKR
    To From Maximum       1
    To From Minimum       0
    To From Name          is for

    ASSOCIATION           TYPE                    NAME

    Is Involved in        Subject Area            Logical Data Model
```
- -
```
Relationship Type: Margin.has.Credit Status

    PROPERTY              VALUE

    Created               1992/11/03 19:51:44 BKR
    From To Maximum       M
    From To Minimum       1
    Last Update           1992/11/03 19:51:44 BKR
    To From Maximum       1
    To From Minimum       0
    To From Name          is for

    ASSOCIATION           TYPE                    NAME

    Is Involved in        Subject Area            Logical Data Model
```
- -
```
Relationship Type: Security.is bought or sold by.Activity

    PROPERTY              VALUE

    Created               1992/11/03 19:49:19 BKR
    From To Maximum       M
    From To Minimum       0
    Last Update           1992/11/03 19:49:19 BKR
    To From Maximum       1
    To From Minimum       0
    To From Name          buys or sells

    ASSOCIATION           TYPE                    NAME

    Is Involved in        Subject Area            Logical Data Model
```

Notes about ADW Output

1. Entities are represented by a rectangle. A small plus sign in the bottom left corner means that additional data about the entity can be obtained by double clicking on the entity with the mouse.

2. A single line is used for a relationship. The line does not need to be labeled, but it can be labeled in one or both directions. Membership class is represented by the use of "0," "1," and "n" or, optionally, by crow's-feet. All relationships are binary.

3. Associative entities are designated using the standard diamond in a box.

4. A black triangle in the lower right corner of the entity box designates a supertype.

5. Subtypes have a black triangle in the upper left corner of the entity.

6. There is no special symbol for exclusion.

7. Attributive entities are depicted by using only the top half of a diamond in the entity box.

8. Recursion is represented by adding a unary relationship to the entity.

LBMS (Learmonth and Burchett Management Systems)
1800 West Loop South
Suite 1800
Houston, TX 77027
Phone (713) 623-0414 and (800) 231-7515
FAX (713) 623-4955

Product: LBMS Systems Engineer

Release 4.01 was used for the business case.

Systems Engineer, a full life cycle–integrated CASE tool, is a client/server application available in single-user and multiuser configurations. The single-user configuration requires a minimum of a 386 20-MHz PC with 4 to 6 MB of RAM. The multiuser configuration requires a dedicated database server, typically a 486 33-MHz PC with 8 to 16 MB of RAM. Multiple client workstations (same requirements as a single-user workstation) communicate with the database servers through Net BIOS across a local area network. The user interface is Windows 3.x.

Besides data modeling, Systems Engineer supports process modeling (data flow diagrams) to nine levels, a number of rapid application development techniques such as screen painting, pull-down menu-assisted pseudo code generation, database schema generation, and code generation (using Micro Focus COBOL Workbench).

DBMSs supported are DB2, Sybase, SQL server, Gupta, Oracle, Ingres, XDB and ANSI SQL. Systems Engineer can generate code for IBM mainframe, AS/400 and PC hardware, DEC, ICL, Unisys, and NCR Unix platforms.

A hypertext subsystem allows access to documentation on Systems Engineer, LSDM, or SSADM methodologies.

Using the Tool

Each entity must have a unique identifier. Relationships can be represented by foreign keys if desired; however, if foreign keys are used, many-to-many relationships are not allowed. Attributive and associative entities are also supported.

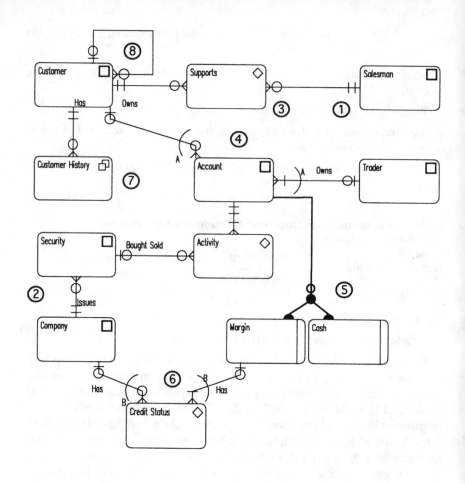

LBMS

02/Dec/1992   01:15PM

Database: WWW40

Page: 1

General Form Full Report

Ref   DMCASE   **Name**   DM / CASE Tool Business Case

Form Type   **Ref** BusCase   **Name**   Business Case

Associated document
Path   c:\winword
Name   sseas   **Type**   doc

Status   Complete

Owning Group   All

Current Version

Created   **Author**   KJF   Updated   **Author**   KJF
          Date/Time   01/Dec/1992 12:28PM   **Date/Time**   02/Dec/1992 01:13PM

*** End of General Form Full Report ***

‡‡LBMS

01/Dec/1992 05:49PM

Database: WWW40   Page: 1

Data Model - South Seas Company Entity Report

Name   Customer

    Class   Kernel   **Access Entry Point**   No

Description

    An outside person, persons, or organization we currently provide professional services to , or provided services in
    the past, or potentially will provide services inthe near future.

Volumetrics

    Volumes
      Minimum   1400000   **Average**   1700000   **Maximum**   2000000
      Length   98

    Volatility
      Inserts   75000   **Updates**   100000   **Deletes**   5000
      Reads   5000000   **Period**   Year

    Comment

    Customer occurrences cannot be deleted within one year of the last activity or if there is a debit balance.

    Growth Rate: 7 percent annually

Created   **Author** KJF   **Updated**   **Author** KJF
            Date/Time 01/Dec/1992 10:22AM   **Date/Time** 01/Dec/1992 05:44PM

Attributes

    Customer Name Occurs 1
      Type: 1:1 Percent: 100
    Customer Address Occurs 1
      Type: 1:1 Percent: 100
    Customer Type Occurs 1
      Type: 1:1 Percent: 100
    Customer Number Occurs 1
      Type: 1:1 Percent: 100
    o Foreign Resident Code Occurs 1
      Type: 0:1 Percent: 6

Keys

    Type   **Name**
    Primary   Primary Key

        Asc   Customer Name

*** End of Entity Report ***

#LBMS
01/Dec/1992 06:00PM

Database: WWW40   Page: 1

Data Item Report

Name Customer Number

      Status   Complete

Description

    A six digit integer assigned sequentially by the Credit Dept. to uniquely identify a customer.

Logical

Class	Identifier
Units	
Length	6
Default	

Storage: Type

Format	Integer				
Length	6	**Precision**		**Signed**	No

Storage: Database Values

    Default
    If Null
    FieldProc

Validation

Minimum	100001	**Maximum**	899999
Value Set			

    Error Code
    Message(s)

    Description   Positive_number

Information Manager

    Version Number
    Owning Group All

Created	**Author**	SYSMGR	**Updated**	**Author**	KJF
	Date/Time	19/May/1992 01:12AM		**Date/Time**	01/Dec/1992 11:48AM

Synonyms

    <u>Name</u>
    Client Id
    Client Number
    Customer Id

■■LBMS
02/Dec/1992   01:24PM

Database: WWW40   Page: 4

Data Model - South Seas Company Relationship Report

Master Entity

    Name   Customer   **Class** Kernel

  Cardinality
    Maximum   One   **Minimum**   Zero   **Exclusive Set**

Relationship Names

    Master to Detail   Owns
    Detail to Master

Detail Entity

    Name   Account   **Class** Kernel

  Cardinality
    Maximum   Many   **Minimum**   Zero   **Exclusive Set**   A

Description

    A customer owns zero or more accounts. Ownership implies a legal ownership status.

Master Volumetrics

  Volumes
    Minimum   15000   **Average**   20000   **Maximum**   25000

  Volatility
    Inserts   750   **Deletes**   100
    Period   Year

  Comment

Detail Volumetrics

  Volumes
    Minimum   0   **Average**   1.2   **Maximum**   99999999.99

  Volatility
    Inserts   **Deletes**
    Period

  Comment

Referential Integrity

      Delete Master   Delete Details
  Update Master Key   Update Foreign Keys
     Insert Detail   Master Must Exist

Notes about Systems Engineer Output

1. Entities are represented by a rounded rectangle. A proper or fundamental entity has a small square in the upper right corner.

2. A single line is used for a relationship. Membership class is represented by the use of crow's-feet.

3. Associative entities are identified by a small diamond in the upper right corner of the entity box.

4. Supertypes are standard proper entity boxes (i.e., they have a small square in the upper right corner) but are identified by a relationship line intersected by a black circle.

5. Subtypes have a single vertical line on the right side of the entity box.

6. Exclusion is represented by a curved line or arc through the relationship.

7. Attributive entities have two small squares in the upper right corner of the entity box.

8. Recursion is represented by a unary relationship line.

Logic Works Inc.
214 Carnegie Center
Suite 112
Princeton, NJ 08540
Phone (609) 243-0088
FAX (609) 243-9192

Product: ERwin

ERwin is a database design tool that supports a different approach to data modeling than the one discussed in this book. Rather than the Entity-Relationship approach, ERwin is based on the IDEF1X model developed by Robert Brown in 1979. Even dyed-in-the-wool E-R modelers might have to deal with IDEF1X, since it is the standard for the U.S. Air Force and growing in popularity. Though of a different lineage than E-R tools, ERwin and the other CASE products share many similarities, such as the emphasis on entities, attributes, and relationships. Nevertheless, differences are also apparent.

IDEF1X is closely tied to the relational model. The "complete" data model requires that entities have primary keys for identification and foreign keys to define relationships. All relationships are binary, with many-to-many relationships being resolved into two one-to-many relationships through the introduction of an intersection entity. In the process of creating the model, however, early versions can have a more "E-R" flavor in that keys (primary and foreign) are not required and many-to-many relationships are allowed.

ERwin runs under Windows, Macintosh, and Unix Motif based products and emphasizes the use of other tools as the delivery vehicle for its reporting. For example, word processors such as Microsoft Word and spreadsheets such as Excel can be used to print ERwin reports, or reports can be printed directly by ERwin (as the enclosed were).

Recommended hardware for Windows 3.x is a 386 with 2-MB RAM, VGA monitor, and 5 MB of disk. For the MAC, System 7 with 4 MB of RAM.

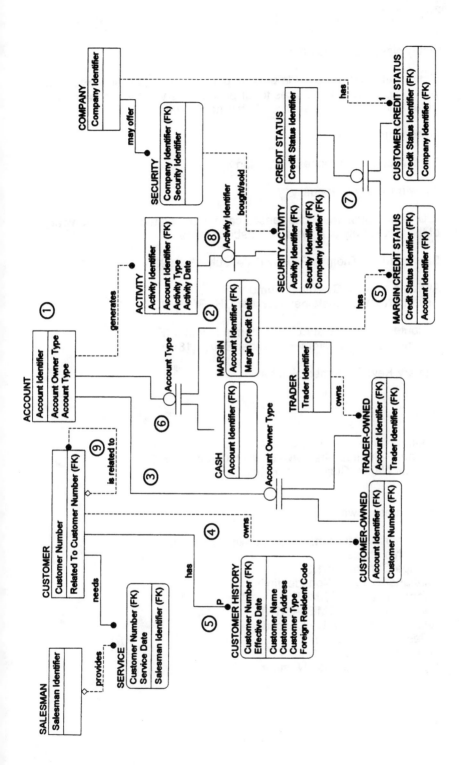

217

Entity Name: CUSTOMER

Entity Definition: An outside person, persons, or organization we currently provide professional services to, or provided services in the past, or potentially will provide services in the near future.

Synonyms: Client

Entity Note: Occurrences 1.4 million

Growth Rate: 7% annually

IUD Rules: Customer occurrences cannot be deleted within one year of the last activity or if there is a debit balance.

Submitted by: Thomas Rowley Date: July 16, 1992

Attribute Names: Customer Number (PK)
Column Names: Customer_Number CHAR(18) NOT NULL

Attribute Names: Related To Customer Number (FK)
Column Names: Customer_Number CHAR(18)

Primary Key: Customer_Number

Domain Name: VALID_CUST_NUM
Domain Rule: integers between 100001 and 899999
Attribute Name: Customer Number

Verb Phrase: owns

Relationship Definition: Ownership implies a legal
ownership status.
Average Cardinality: 1,2
Relationship Type: Non-identifying
Parent Entity: CUSTOMER
Child Entity: CUSTOMER-OWNED
Referential Integrity: U - Cascade
I - Restrict   D - Set Null
Logical FK: Customer Number
Physical FK: Customer_Number

Attribute Name: Customer Name
Attribute Type: Owned Non-key
Base Name: Customer Name
Schema Datatype: CHAR(25)
Entity Usage: CUSTOMER HISTORY

Attribute Name: Customer Number
Attribute Definition: A six digit integer assigned sequentially
by the Credit Dept. to uniquely identify a customer

Synonyms: Customer ID, Client ID, Client Number
Attribute Type: Owned Key
Base Name: Customer Number
Schema Datatype: CHAR(18)
Entity Usage: CUSTOMER
PK: (PK)
Null Option: NOT NULL

Attribute Name: Customer Number
Attribute Type: Foreign Key
Base Name: Customer Number
Schema Datatype: INTEGER
Entity Usage: CUSTOMER HISTORY
FK: (FK)
PK: (PK)
Null Option: NOT NULL

Notes about ERwin Output

1. Independent entities are entities which do not rely on other entities for their existence. They are represented by a rectangle with squared corners.

2. Dependent entities, which need other entities for their identification, share the independent entity's primary key. Dependent entities are represented by a rectangle with rounded corners.

3. Identifying relationships, where the subordinate entity inherits its key from the independent entity, are represented with a solid line. These relationships are mandatory.

4. A dotted line is used to denote a nonidentifying relationship. The "dependent" entity might still store the primary key of the parent entity, but it is not used to uniquely identify the child. This relationship can be optional.

5. The dot indicates a cardinality of many. The letter "P" added to the relationship line indicates that the cardinality is one or more, while a "Z" indicates that it is zero or one. A number on the line indicates the exact number of occurrences.

6. Generalizations (subtypes) are supported with a rather unique symbol consisting of a circle with one or two lines beneath it. A "complete category structure," sometimes called a closed subtype, occurs when all of the subtypes of a supertype are known and displayed. Complete category structures are depicted by a circle with two lines under it.

7. Exclusion is not specifically supported. In our diagram it is treated as a subtype construct.

8. An open subtype, or an "incomplete category structure," indicates that only some of the possible subtypes are known or displayed. A circle with a single line under it is used to indicate an incomplete category structure.

9. The diamond shows that the nonidentifying relationship is optional. A relationship without the diamond indicates the relationship is mandatory.

Popkin Software & Systems Incorporated
11 Park Place
New York, NY 10007
Phone (212) 571-3434
FAX (212) 571-3436

Product: System Architect

Version 2.4 was used for the business case.

System Architect, a PC-based CASE product, requires 2 MB RAM for the Windows 3.x version and 4 MB for the OS/2 PM 2.0 version. Both require 5 MB for the disk. Actual memory and disk storage usage may vary based on project and diagram size and PC configuration.

System Architect supports the Chen and IDEF1X data modeling approaches and incorporates various display options, such as whether to represent cardinality with crow's-feet, arrows, or letters and numbers. The tool does not require that every entity have a unique identifier or that relationships be defined using a foreign key. It does support N-ary and many-to-many relationships as well as associative and attributive entities.

The user can define new data dictionary entries for data objects. So, if your favorite data item is not explicitly represented in the dictionary, you can add the field yourself.

Other techniques supported

System Architect also supports various approaches to process modeling (data flow diagramming and state transition diagrams) and a number of object-oriented modeling approaches.

Downstream activity includes a data normalization tool, structure charts, and several database schema generators including those for the AS/400, ANSI SQL, DB2, Informix, Ingres, Oracle, OS/2 Database Manager, Paradox, Rdb, SQL Base, SQL Server, XDB, and Progress. A reverse data engineering tool will be out shortly. It will allow the generation of a data model from a database schema.

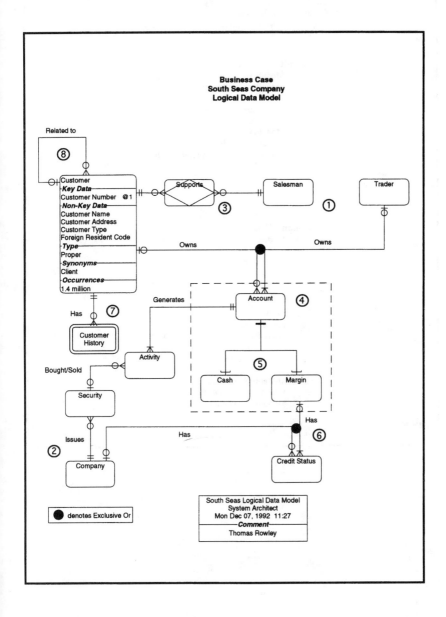

South Seas Company
Relationship Definition

Relationship Name: Customer/Account   **Type:** Binary
Description:
A customer owns zero or more accounts. Ownership implies a legal ownership status.

From entity: Customer
Modality/Cardinality: Zero, One or Many
Modality/Cardinality: Zero, One or Many
Modality/Cardinality: Zero, One or Many
Average: 1.2   **Max:** Unlimited   **Min:** Zero

To entity: Account
Modality/Cardinality: Only One
Modality/Cardinality: Zero or One
Notes:
Submitted by:

Modality/Cardinality:
Modality/Cardinality:
Modality/Cardinality: Zero or One
Notes:
Submitted by:

To entity: Trader
Modality/Cardinality: Zero or One
Notes:
Submitted by:

To entity: Account
Modality/Cardinality: Only One
Modality/Cardinality: Zero or One
Notes:
Submitted by:

Modality/Cardinality:
Modality/Cardinality:
Modality/Cardinality: Zero or One

South Seas Company
Entity Definition

Name: Customer   **Entity Type:** Proper
Short Description:
An outside person, persons, or organization we currently provide professional services to, or provided services in the past, or potentially will provide services in the near future.

Synonyms: Client
Occurrences: 1.4 million
Growth Rate:
7 percent annually

Notes (IUD Rules, etc):
Customer occurrences cannot be deleted within one year of the last activity or if there is a debit balance.

Submitted by: Thomas Rowley   12/01/92
    Name: *Customer Number*   **Attribute Type:** *Identifier*
    Domain Definition:
    A six-character integer between 100001 and 899999

    Format: 6I
    Length: 6
    Acceptable Values:
    Integers between 100001 and 899999

    Domain submitted by: Thomas Rowley
    Name: *Customer Name*   **Attribute Type:** *Name*
    Domain Definition:

    Format:
    Length: 5
    Acceptable Values:

    Domain submitted by:
    Name: *Customer Address*   **Attribute Type:** *Description*
    Domain Definition:

    Format:
    Length: 5
    Acceptable Values:

    Domain submitted by:
    Name: *Customer Type*   **Attribute Type:** *Code*

**South Seas Company
Domain Definition**

Name: Customer Number
Description:
A six-character integer between 100001 and 899999

Length: 6
Format: 6I
Abbreviations:

Validation Rules:
Default Values:

Acceptable Values:
Integers between 100001 and 899999

Notes:

Submitted by: Thomas Rowley   12/01/92

South Seas Company
Attribute Definition

Name: Customer Number
Attribute Type: Identifier
List Process Name if Attribute Type is Derived:
Description:
A six-digit integer assigned sequentially by the Credit Dept. to uniquely identify a customer.

Synonyms: "Customer ID" "Client ID" "Client Number"
Domain: Customer Number
Size: 6I
Notes:
Domain Definition:
A six-character integer between 100001 and 899999

Format: 6I
Length: 6
Acceptable Values:
Integers between 100001 and 899999

Submitted by: Thomas Rowley   12/01/92

Notes about System Architect Output

1. All entities are represented with a rounded rectangle.

2. Relationships are shown with a straight line. Crow's-feet are used to represent membership class.

3. The associative entity is represented by the common diamond in an entity box.

4. Generalization is depicted with the entities in a rectangle drawn with a dotted line. The supertype is connected to the subtypes with a line bisected by a single bold cardinality bar.

5. Subtypes are also depicted in the dotted-lined box and connected to the supertype with a line bisected by a single U-shaped cardinality bar. The only way to differentiate the supertype from the subtype is by the type of cardinality bar—bold for the supertype and U-shaped for the subtype.

6. Exclusion is represented by a black circle drawn through the exclusive relationships.

7. Attributive entities are denoted with a double-lined entity box. Version 3.0, to be released soon, will allow a choice of a double box or a single-lined box surrounding the top half of a diamond.

8. Recursion is represented with a single unary relationship line.

B

At a Glance: Principles, Guidelines, and Rules of Thumb

"That's not a regular rule: you invented it just now." LEWIS CARROLL

"Let us not be too particular. It is better to have old secondhand diamonds than none at all." MARK TWAIN

Principles

The communication principle

Foster communication of business requirements to technical staff and end users alike. Requirements must be clearly stated so as to be understandable by all audiences, end-user-oriented, and consist of detail that illuminates.

The granularity principle

Represent a low granularity of data and present a "lowest common denominator" of the structure of the information that the organization uses. Complicated structures should be broken down into their elementary parts, and unnecessary structure and duplication removed.

The logical representation principle

Present a logical view of the organization's data. The model should reflect a business orientation without physical constraints. Physical design options should be left open. The logical data model should not be tied to a particular architecture, technology, or product.

Guidelines

Abbreviations should be kept to a minimum, and when used, they should be meaningful to the end user.

Clarity   Remove confusing objects from the data model.

Compound identifiers are acceptable, and the position of the attributes within an identifier is unimportant.

Conceptual integrity   Maintain the integrity of logical data modeling concepts, even if the tool you are using makes it difficult.

Conjunctive relationships   Allow conjunctive *or and* relationships, since they are a legitimate end-user concept.

Data value differentiated entities and attributes   Do not allow data values to differentiate or define entities or other attributes.

Data Values   Do not model the values of data.

Avoid placing *derived data* on the data model, though it should be in the data dictionary.

Discrete attributes   An attribute should exist in the model once and only once.

Do not allow *embedded attributes*.

Empty entities   When the data model is finished, no entities should exist without attributes, nor should they have only one attribute in them (especially if the one attribute is a code or an indicator) or only identifiers.

Exclusive relationships   Allow *exclusive or* either/or relationships, since they are a legitimate end-user concept.

Avoid *extraneous relationships*.

Although perhaps unavoidable with some tools, defining relationships through *foreign keys* should be discouraged.

Group data items are to be avoided, since they can hide information about attributes and entity relationships.

Identifiers   The designation of one or more attributes as an entity identifier is encouraged and should be specified if the identifier is a legitimate end-user concept. However, "assigning" an identifier or arbitrarily making one identifier "primary" for systems purposes is wrong and should be discouraged.

Level of abstraction   Make the data model as abstract as possible while still fully and adequately describing the subject.

Allow a *many-to-many (M:N) relationship* if the relationship does not have any attributes of its own.

Naming objects   Data object names should be meaningful, yet follow some uniform approach or standard when possible. Avoid naming conventions that aim simply at control, yet fail to communicate.

N-ary relationships   Relationships can legitimately exist between two, three, or more entities.

Normalization   Normalize data models where possible, but do not break any logical data modeling best practices to do so.

Null attributes are perfectly acceptable, but they should be scrutinized carefully and dependence on them should be discouraged. (Make sure they are not the result of combining multiple entities or subtypes into one.)

Allow *optional relationships*.   (Optional-optional relationships)

Presentation data   Do not model reports, transactions, screens, or views.

Primary keys   The designation of one or more identifiers for an entity is encouraged, but not required. The specification of one of the unique keys as the "primary key" is unnecessary.

Process data   Do not model process data, data flows, triggers, formulas, policy, rules, or the passing of control.

Do not allow *repeating groups*, since they can hide entity and relationship data.

Allow *subject areas*.

Do not model *substitution data* unless it is necessary for understanding the business.

The use of *supertypes and subtypes* is acceptable.

Do not model *transient data*, since it is usually temporary, duplicate, or process related.

Rules of Thumb

Identify *"almost unique" identifiers* when known, since they can be useful for application development.

Be wary of *associatives related to other associatives*, since in a correct model they are somewhat rare.

Circular relationships are impossible.

Diagrammable objects   Not all data objects should be represented on the diagram of the logical data model. Carefully review all data objects to determine which ones should be part of the model.

Disassociated entity clusters ("islands")   Since legitimate disassociated entities and entity clusters are rare, their occurrence on the model most often reflects incorrectly modeled data.

Duplicate identifiers   Although it is not uncommon or wrong for two entities to share an attribute as their identifiers, the practice should be discouraged.

Duplicate sub-supertype "type" data   A duplicate "type" attribute is appropriate in subtype entities.

Entity fragmentation   Avoid unnecessarily fragmenting entities.

Junction entities   The use of junction records should not be confused with the role of legitimate associative entities.

Multiple relationships   If more than two or three relationships exist between two entities, you may want to show only one relationship and describe in the relationship definition all the possible relationships.

One of a kind (OOAK) entities   Try to avoid modeling OOAKs.

One-to-one relationships, while legitimate, are quite rare.

Rare entity relationships   Certain entity/relationships simply do not occur that often. When they appear on the model, they should be investigated.

Check all *recursive relationships*, since they are the most likely to be incorrectly modeled. Specifically, check for incorrect *modality* and *cardinality*.

Single attribute entities   An entity should have more than one attribute in it.

"Spiderwebs" are usually the sign of an immature data model or incorrectly defined relationships.

Avoid linking *substitution tables* to other entities.

Symmetrical models, relationships, attributes   Be on the lookout for symmetrical models, since they probably represent an incorrect or immature data model.

Be careful of *too many nulls* in an entity. They might indicate incorrectly defined entities.

Be careful of *too many recursive relationships*, which often reflect the efforts of an inexperienced data modeler.

Data Modeling Reading List

"If I have seen further it is by standing on the shoulders of giants."   ISAAC NEWTON

"We can lick gravity, but the paperwork is overwhelming."   WERNHER VON BRAUN

Books

S. Atre, *Data Base: Structured Techniques for Design, Performance, and Measurement.* John Wiley & Sons, 1980. *A good discussion of normalization.*

Thomas A. Bruce, *Designing Quality Databases with IDEF1X Information Models.* Dorset House Publishing, 1992. *This book offers the best description of the IDEF1X data modeling methodology.*

Peter P. Chen (ed), *Entity Relationship Approach to Systems Analysis and Design.* North Holland, 1980. *A collection of papers on entity modeling, most from the Entity Relationship Institute's annual conferences. Unfortunately this work is difficult to find.*

Peter P. Chen, *The Entity Relationship Approach to Logical Data Base Design.* QED Information Systems, Inc., 1977. *An expanded version of Chen's 1976 paper.*

Chen and Associates, Inc., *ER Designer* (user manual), 1987. *The guide for using the Chen data modeling product. It also gives an excellent though short overview of Chen's approach to data modeling.*

Candace C. Fleming, and Barbara Von Halle, *Handbook of Relational Database Design.* Addison Wesley, 1989. *Good discussion of normalization.*

G. M. Nijssen and T. A. Halpan, *Conceptual Schema and Relational Database Design.* Prentice Hall, 1989. *Probably the best explanation of NIAM (Nijssen's Information Analysis Methodology). Encompassing both process and data modeling, NIAM is a particularly popular approach in Europe.*

Toby J. Teorey, *Database Modeling and Design: The Entity Relationship Approach,* Morgan Kaufman Publishers, Inc., 1990. *Encompasses the 1989 Teorey ACM paper and also goes into physical design issues.*

Articles

Peter P. Chen, "The Entity Relationship Model—Toward a Unified View of Data," *ACM Transactions,* Database Systems, 1(1): 9–36, March 1976. *The paper that introduced the entity relationship approach. Good for historical value, though more recent works present concepts beyond this paper, and some do a better job describing the E-R model.*

Peter P. Chen, "English Sentence Structure and Entity-Relationship Diagrams," *Information Sciences*, 29: 127–149, 1983. *The classic paper on translating English syntax into data modeling constructs. Concepts from this paper also appear in the Chen Associates ER Designer (user manual).*

D. Reiner, M. Brodie, G. Brown, M. Friedll, D. Kvamlich, J. Lechmanand, and A. Rosenthal, "The Data Base Design and Evaluation Workbench (DDEW) Project at CCA," *Database Engineering*, 7(4): 10–15, 1985. *The paper that introduced the diagramming conventions used by McFlow and Symbol Sampler.*

T. J. Teorey, G. Wei, D. L. Bolton, and J. A. Koenig, "ER Model Clustering as an Aid for User Concepts and Documentation in Database Design," *Communications of the ACM* 32(8): 975–987, August 1989. *An excellent description of Reiner et al.'s 1985 paper.*

Glossary

Abstraction   A representation of a subject that excludes unnecessary detail while focusing on important features.

Analysis   See **Logical Design**

Association   In object-oriented development, a natural or business relationship between objects.

Associative Entity   A relationship that has its own properties or attributes.

Asymmetrical Relationship   A unidirectional unary relationship which represents a sequence or hierarchy that must have a beginning and end. Asymmetrical relationships cannot be mandatory.

Attribute   A property of an entity such as COLOR, NAME, EMPLOYMENT DATE, SOCIAL SECURITY NUMBER.

Attributive Entity   An entity whose existence depends on another entity.

Best Practices   An experience-based collection of rules, advice, and insight regarding the correct, most effective, and/or productive application of one or more techniques. (In this book, best practices are the principles, guidelines, and "rules of thumb" that provide data modelers with practical information to aid them in the modeling process.)

Binary Relationship   A relationship involving just two entities.

Cardinality   The maximum number of occurrences of one entity type, usually expressed as simply "one" or "many," that can be related to a number of occurrences of another entity type.

Class   See **Object Class**

Compound Identifier   An identifier consisting of more than one attribute.

Computer-Aided Software Engineering (CASE)   A software product, usually divided into upper CASE and lower CASE, consisting of a number of different tools that automate part of the system development process. Upper CASE includes automated aids for performing system development techniques such as data and process modeling tools. Lower CASE is more concerned with code generators and testing tools. CASE tools that include both upper and lower CASE are sometimes called integrated CASE or ICASE.

Conjunction   Two related relationships between three entities, e.g., if entity type 'A' is related to entity type 'B,' it must also be related to entity type 'C.' Conjunction is also called an *and* relationship.

Data Aggregate   See **Group Data Item**

Data Dictionary   A mechanism to store information about automated systems which can be as simple as a directory of data element names, formats, and locations in files or as robust as a repository for all the documentation dealing with the development or operation of a system. The dictionary can be in a loose-leaf binder or a sophisticated automated system. A data dictionary that stores process and operational information is sometimes called an information repository.

Data Element   See **Primitive Attribute**

Data Model   A model representing the definition, characterization, and relationships of data in an environment. See also **Logical Data Model** and **Physical Database Design.**

Data Modeling   The process of identifying and representing the definition, usage, and/or storage of data, usually to build or document a physical data repository.

Data Modeling Objects   The building blocks of a data model. The three basic objects are entities, attributes, and relationships.

Data Repository   See **Data Dictionary**

Data Service Request   Used in physical database design, a request to the information manager for access to the database.

Data Service Request Map   The diagram produced when Data Service Requests are graphically mapped to the physical database design.

Database Design   See **Physical Database Design**

Database Management System (DBMS)   A software system to manage the storage, access, and update of information for one or many users.

Degree   The number of entities in a relationship, i.e., whether the relationship is unary, binary, or n-ary.

Derived Data   An attribute whose value can be calculated from one or more atomic facts or other derived attributes by the application of an algorithm. For example, INVOICE AMOUNT is derived if its value can be calculated by summing the ITEM AMOUNT values.

Descriptor Attribute   A not necessarily unique property or characteristic of an entity or relationship (associative entity) instance, e.g., COLOR = "blue."

Design   See **Physical Design**

Detailed Logical Data Model   A complete logical data model, often application oriented, providing a view of the organization's entities, relationships, and attributes. The detailed data model is the principal tool for communicating data between the analysts and database designers and should contain a complete specification of all relevant information about the organization's data.

Domain   A set of possible values of an attribute type, e.g., "July 11, 1983," is an acceptable value for EMPLOYMENT DATE.

Embedded Attribute   An attribute with multiple facts "buried" inside; e.g., ACCOUNT NUMBER might be made up of the data items "branch code" and a "sequence number within branch."

Encapsulation   In object-oriented development, the principle that the attributes and operations of an object are hidden to other objects and that what goes on inside an object is not related to what might be going on outside the object.

End-User Logical Data Model   A data model, often "enterprise" oriented, that represents a high-level end-user view usually developed during planning or at the very beginning of analysis. It includes only the basic entities and relationships with examples of attributes. Attributes uncovered while building the end-user model will probably be representative or examples. Modelers sometimes use the phrase "such as" to indicate that the entity will contain information such as account type, tax classification, etc.

End Users   Those who commission the building of an information system, represent those who commission the system, or will use the system commissioned. They are usually nontechnical staff (unless the system is designed to serve technical staff, e.g., an application tracking system).

Enterprise Model   A model, or series of models, that describe(s) an entire organization or enterprise. There are usually two enterprise models, an enterprise process model and an enterprise data model.

Enterprise Data Model   A logical data model of an entire organization or enterprise. An enterprise data model is usually a high-level model, often at a higher level than an end-user logical data model.

Entity   A person, place, or thing about which an organization wishes to save information, e.g., Employees, States, Orders, and Time Sheets.

Entity Fragment Diagram   A view or portion of the data model that deals with a specific process or processes.

Entity-Relationship Approach (Entity-Relationship Model)   An approach to logical data modeling introduced by Peter Chen in 1976 that focuses on the nontechnical "business" data objects, entities, attributes, and relationships rather than on files, records, and databases.

Entity-Relationship Diagram   The logical data modeling diagram; part of the output and the graphic representation of the entity-relationship approach.

Exclusion   Two associated relationships between three entities where entity type 'A' can be related to entity type 'B' or to entity type 'C,' but not both (also known as an *exclusive or* relationship).

Extended Entity-Relationship Approach   A series of extensions to the E-R model to expand its functionality (e.g., supertypes and subtypes).

Facilitated Joint Session   An alternative to the standard one-on-one interview for analyzing applications, the facilitated joint session consists of a formal meeting of a number of users and analysts to develop, in the span of a few days, the complete analysis of a system, or subsystem.

Foreign Key(s)   In relational theory, one or more fields in one table that consist of the same definition(s) and domain(s) as the primary key in another table. Foreign keys are used for linking related tables together.

Generalization/Specialization   See **Supertypes and Subtypes**

Group Data Item   A number of related attributes (such as CUSTOMER STREET, CUSTOMER CITY, CUSTOMER STATE, and CUSTOMER POSTAL CODE) linked together with a common name (such as CUSTOMER ADDRESS).

Guideline   An agreed upon set of rules that, once adopted, should be followed by all.

Identifier   An attribute that uniquely determines an entity or relationship instance, e.g., EMPLOYEE NUMBER can uniquely identify an employee.

Inclusion   Two associated relationships between three entities where entity 'A' can be related to entity 'B' or to entity 'C' or to both (also known as an *inclusive or* relationship).

Inheritance   The transference of the properties of one data object to another data object. In data modeling, subtypes can inherit attributes and relationships from the supertype. In object-oriented modeling, an object can inherit attributes, relationships, and behavior from its superclass.

Instance   See **Occurrence**

IUD Anomaly   A data integrity problem that occurs when an insert, update, or delete occurring in one area of the database adversely affects a data object in another area.

Logical Data Model   A model of the information used in an organization from an end-user perspective without regard to its functional or physical aspects.

Logical Data Modeling   A collection, verification, and communication technique to fully document data requirements to aid in the development of accurate, efficient, and flexible physical information platforms (databases or file structures).

Logical Design   The phase in the system development life cycle in which the user's view of the application is documented in terms of *what* the user wants, not *how* it will be delivered, and which becomes the input to the physical design phase.

Membership Class   The cardinality and modality of a relationship.

Message   The means of communication between objects in object-oriented development.

Method   See **Operation**

Methodology   An approach to applying one or more techniques that usually includes the sequence of steps to be performed, deliverables to be produced, discipline to be followed, and project management steps to be executed.

Modality   The modality of a relationship indicates whether an entity occurrence must participate in a relationship. Modality (also called **optionality**) tells you the minimum number of occurrences, while cardinality tells you the maximum number of occurrences of an entity that can participate in a relationship.

Model   An abstract representation of a subject that looks and/or behaves like part or all of the original. The model can be physical, such as a mockup of the space shuttle, a drawing, or blueprint, or conceptual, such as the mathematical formulas used for weather forecasting.

Modeling   The process of creating the abstract representation of a subject so that it can be studied more cheaply (a scale model of an airplane in a wind tunnel), or at a particular moment in time (weather forecasting), or manipulated, modified, and altered without disrupting the original (economic models).

Multi-Valued Attribute   An attribute with more than one value, such as a customer with multiple addresses.

N-ary Relationship   A relationship involving more than two entity types, e.g., in 'Customer Buys a Car from a Dealer,' Customer, Car, and Dealer are all entities linked by the common relationship 'Buy.'

Neighborhood Diagram   A data model fragment showing one entity at a time with only its relationships and the entities that are tied to those relationships.

Normalization   A physical database design technique involving the application of a set of mathematical rules to the data model to identify and reduce insertion, update, or deletion (IUD) anomalies.

Null Value   An attribute that has no value.

Object Instance   An occurrence of an object class, i.e., if Employer is an object class, "Thomas Chatterton" is an object instance.

Object Class   In object-oriented development, a group of objects that share data types and behavior.

Object-Oriented Analysis   An approach to analyzing applications that centers around the study of business objects.

Object-Oriented Development   The generic name for any of a series of object-oriented approaches to systems development (including methodologies, analysis, design, modeling, programming, and database management systems). It is based on the premise that systems consist of semi-autonomous objects and the communications between them. Proponents believe that constructing systems consistent with this model will foster structured design and code reuse.

Occurrence   A single case or instance of a type, e.g., 'Socrates' represents a single occurrence or 'type' of 'Man.'

Operation   An algorithm that makes up part of an object in object-oriented development and is used to access, create, delete, or modify one or more attributes.

Optionality   See **Modality**.

Physical Database Design   A data model configured to reflect the usage of data for a particular physical environment. The DBMS or language dependent specifications of what the information base should look like and how it should function. A process for identifying and evaluating tradeoffs and calculating the best all-around solutions that balance performance and cost for current and near-term needs of the end user.

Physical Design   The phase in the system development life cycle where the user's view of the application is converted into technical design specifications with emphasis on *how* to deliver *what* the user wants.

Presentation Data   Copies of existing modeled attributes or derived from modeled attributes and used in reports or on terminal screens but not included on the data model.

Primary Key   A field (or multiple fields) that in physical data modeling functions as an identifier in a record type and is used as the principal method of physically locating a record for storage or access.

Primitive Attribute   An attribute whose value expresses an atomic or lowest level fact about the entity, as in the COLOR is "blue."

Proper Entity   A simple or fundamental entity.

Recursive Relationship   See **Unary Relationship**

Relational Database Management System (RDBMS)   A DBMS based on the relational model.

Relational Model   A set theoretic representation of data and data operators which presents data as two-dimensional arrays.

Relationship   A verb that describes how entities are naturally linked to each other, as in 'Customers Buy Products,' 'Employees File Time Sheets,' 'Sales Representatives Place Orders.' *Note*: When data modelers talk about a "relationship," they mean an end-user relationship, not a technical one.

Relationship Entity Pair   A sentence construct ('Entity Relationship Entity') that represents a binary relationship.

Relationship Constraint   A restriction, namely, exclusion, inclusion, or conjunction, on one or more relationships. Relationships can be linked in a way that the occurrence of one relationship can affect the occurrence of another.

Repository   See **Data Dictionary**

Rules of Thumb   Best practices that should be followed even though they do not have the strength of a guideline or rule. They often indicate what is usually, but not universally, applicable to a model or situation.

Semantic Data Model   See **Extended Entity-Relationship Approach**

Structure Chart   A representation of the different software modules that make up programs and how the modules interact.

Structured Analysis   A technique for achieving logical design that typically focuses on a top-down model of the application.

Structured Design A technique for creating programming specifications and code that focuses on top-down design and modularity of code.

Subject Area A subset of a data model consisting of related entities and relationships.

Substitution Data Data stored in an abbreviation table that allows the storage of smaller codes (such as Postal Code) in large occurrence record types (such as Customer). When the record is to be accessed, a conversion table is read to fetch the name of the town relating to the postal code.

Supertypes and Subtypes Designations of entities as a collection of related entity roles (supertype) or the role an entity can play (subtype). For example, the supertype Customer can include the subtypes Retail Customer and Wholesale Customer which inherit the attributes and relationships of the supertype but can also have their own attributes and relationships.

Symmetrical Relationship Bi-directional, unary relationships which have no beginning or end and which have a modality of mandatory-mandatory or optional-optional.

Technical Users The system designers who use the output of other system designers.

Technique A series of steps applied to a subject to change its representation. Data modeling, processing modeling, and prototyping are all techniques.

Tool A physical or conceptual product that aids in applying techniques. CASE products and flow charting templates are tools.

Transient Data Temporary, duplicate, or process-related data that is usually not kept by the system or included on the logical data model.

Type A class or set of objects that share a distinguishing factor.

Unary Relationship An entity occurrence related to another entity occurrence of the same entity type. For example, if some employees supervise other employees, then the relationship 'Supervises' is from Employee to Employee.

Value The name given to an attribute instance or occurrence of an attribute type; a characteristic or fact about an entity occurrence.

Weak Entity See **Attributive Entity**

Index

ABOUT THE AUTHOR

George Tillmann is a principal with Booz•Allen &
Hamilton's Information Systems Group, the commercial systems division of this international management consulting
firm. He is the author of numerous articles on data processing management and information management systems,
and has designed some of the largest databases in the
world.